Growing Up Plain
The Journey of a
Public Friend

D1453532

Growing Up Plain

Among Conservative Wilburite Quakers

The Journey of a Public Friend

BY WILMER A. COOPER

Friends United Press
Richmond, Indiana
in cooperation with
Pendle Hill Publications
Wallingford, Pennsylvania

Cover and book design by Julia Jensen

First edition

Published by Friends United Press, Richmond, Indiana in association with Pendle Hill Publications, Wallingford, Pennsylvania.

PRINTED IN THE UNITED STATES OF AMERICA

Library of Congress Cataloging-in-Publication Data

Cooper, Wilmer A. (Wilmer Albert)
    Growing up plain among conservative Wilburite Quakers : the
    Journey of a public friend / by Wilmer A. Cooper.
    Includes bibliographical references and index.
    ISBN 0-944350-44-5
    1. Cooper, Wilmer A. (Wilmer Albert) 2. Ohio Yearly Meeting of
    Friends (Conservative : 1854-) Biography. 3. Quakers—United
    States Biography. I. Title. II. Title: Growing up plain.
    BX7795.C745A3   1999
    289.6'092—dc21
    [B]   99-15856

                                                                CIP

Dedicated to
Willis Hall,
S. Arthur Watson,
E. Raymond Wilson,
Landrum Bolling,
and Alexander Purdy,
each of whom had a
significant influence
on my career.

Contents

87.88
good stuff on
Cr & Calvin
radical Puritans
116-117 - good on
liberal & current
Con. Friends

The 'Plain People'

The term "plain people" is usually applied to Amish, Old Mennonites, and some Church of the Brethren.

Conservative Wilburite Friends historically constitute the "plain people" of Quakerdom.

FOREWORD

by
William and Frances Taber

In this book Wilmer Cooper tells the story of his childhood and youth among Conservative Wilburite Quakers and then of his work in the wider Religious Society of
Friends, as well as presenting his assessment of Conservative
Friends' place in the wider scheme of Quakerism. Like many
other religious leaders of the past, Wilmer had to leave the
sheltering nurture and restrictions of his early religious community in order to be faithful to what it had instilled in him—
integrity and obedience in following the call of God.

His personal story might be divided into two parts—
preparation for the "call" which came to him in the boiler room
of his father's greenhouse, and the way in which he followed
that call for the rest of his life. He describes well the mixed
blessings of the "preparation" of growing up in one of the strictest families in the Conservative Ohio Yearly Meeting of the
1920s and 1930s.

Part of that experience was clearly painful in its restric-
tiveness, but, fortunately for Wilmer and his later work for

wider Quakerism, there were positive elements as well. One key to these positive elements in Wilmer's family, as well as in others we have observed, seems to lie in the degree to which parents were able to communicate to their children the "passion for Truth"[1] which lay behind the restrictive customs and "hedges" of the Wilburite, or Conservative Quaker, way of life. Another was the parents' ability to live in such away that their children might have some nonverbal sense of the reality of the Divine Presence, which, after all, is what the restrictive customs and hedges were meant to protect. We have often observed that people like Wilmer, who were "fortunate" in the way they grew up among Conservative Friends (some were not so fortunate), have what might be called "Quaker optimism" about the goodness of the universe and the world of nature in which God is present. Like Wilmer, they enjoy nature as part of the Divine harmony. And, like Wilmer, they have experienced, at least sometimes as children, a comforting Presence in the meeting for worship.

Two incidents involving other members of Wilmer's family, although not as children, may help to illustrate this. His sister Sara Cooper Stratton, who died in 1996, recalled, "My father and I were conscious of the Lord's beautiful presence, which came home with us from First Day (Sunday) meeting and continued while we sat in the living room. It was time to prepare dinner, but this consciousness was more satisfying than thoughts of food. My father said to me, while I was noticing a serene joy in his countenance, 'Sara, there is nothing I could desire more for thee in this life, than this peace, and that thee might have it in the life to come.'"[2]

As a young man many years earlier, Wilmer's Uncle Cyrus Cooper developed a spiritual friendship with Harry Moore, his brother-in-law. Cyrus recalls that about 1897 or 1898, before they had moved to Ohio, "While living at West Grove

[Pennsylvania] I attended meeting more regularly and became intimate with him, [and] we had many congenial talks. After the consoling evidence of Truth in one of our midweek meetings, Harry and I walked together homeward. As we went along the boardwalk 'Every blade of grass was a song of praise, and all the leaves of the trees did clap their hands for joy.' As we conversed, I was sensible that Harry felt my condition and realized I had found peace, yet conscious that he had not obtained it."[3]

It is worth noting that in the passage quoted above, Cyrus uses the expression "felt my condition." This capacity to "feel" the state or condition of another was and is common among many Conservative Friends, who believe that an ability to have what others might call intuition or hunches comes from the practice of seeking to be open to Divine guidance, whether in waiting worship or in the midst of daily life. As a result of this reliance on "feelings" or inward knowing, some Conservative Friends have not been very articulate in explaining their beliefs to their children or to inquiring newcomers.

Wilmer's memories of his mother's guidance also tenderly illustrate how the Conservative culture—at its best—instilled in its children the need for personal prayerful discernment in all areas of life. Paradoxically, even though a child was generally expected to follow the family rules and to observe the Wilburite cultural "hedges," such parents would seek to turn the child, again and again, to his or her own inward discernment rather than to mindless obedience or mere conformity. We have known families where these graces were not so present, and the results were not so good. "Love is time," someone has said. It is clear that Wilmer's mother did take the time to explain and exemplify as well as she could the vast reaches and the small details of the faith to which she had dedicated her life.

After reading an early draft of this book we were at first disappointed that Wilmer gives so much attention to the documents which stress the theological foundation and the sometimes puritanical emphasis on the "hedges" and restrictions of the Wilburite and Conservative Quaker way. Our initial response may have come because we, like Wilmer, have sought to grow beyond the husks of rigidity, literalism, and fear of change that have at times threatened to smother the living center of Conservative Quakerism. However, after careful re-reading, it is clear to us that Wilmer, through these documents, rightly places Conservative Quakerism as a living stream which reaches back to the spiritual Christian Quakerism so well articulated by Robert Barclay.

Wilmer's study reminds us of how, when the rest of Quakerism rationalized into variations of Orthodox-Gurneyite or Hicksite tendencies, Wilburite/Conservative Friends sought to "conserve" what they understood to be the living dynamic center of a Quakerism that was Christian, Biblical, and open to moment-by-moment governance by and communion with the Living Christ. This double intent explains their use of orthodox language and yet their wariness of over-much emphasis on words and doctrine. They feared that an over-dependence on a form of words could keep one from resting in and depending upon the Spirit that gave forth the Scriptures. During this rationalistic century, Conservative Quakerism, at its best, has walked a razor's edge that combines a faithfulness to the orthodox understanding of the Work of Jesus Christ with the "mystical" or "contemplative" experience of the utter impossibility—and the danger of trying—to limit God with words. Living faithfully and joyously on this razor's edge of continual dependence on the Holy Spirit has been possible—in Conservative Quakerism at its best—when the experience of their waiting worship has been deep, quiet, alive, and nourishing, with and without spoken words. There is such a thing as a "dead" Conservative silence, which fails to be alive because of other Wilburite tendencies such as fear of running ahead of the Inward Guide or an exaggerated sense of unworthiness. These tendencies can get in the way of the Spirit, smothering its work.

Especially in the latter part of this book, Wilmer shows how much change has occurred within the Conservative Quaker world throughout this century, so that, as the twentieth century ends, these Friends often would appear to be very different from what they were in 1900, or even at mid-century in Wilmer's childhood enclave at Middleton, Ohio. Perhaps the greatest change lies in the dramatic shrinkage in membership. In 1900 a Conservative Friend was part of a subculture that connected small (usually rural) enclaves in various parts of this country and Canada and even in Fritchley, England. By mid-century, most of these communities had grown smaller, and some had disappeared or reunited with the yearly meetings from whom they had separated long ago. But overall, Conservative Friends still had a significant sense of "critical mass" and could feel a sense of common community and kinship of soul with one another, whether they visited in one of the enclaves or met at wider Quaker gatherings, universities, or in a great city.

Part of the dramatic loss of membership came about because many of these quietist Quakers went out into the world of action, as Wilmer did, sometimes to engage in professional work or to work actively in the wider Quaker world. Some were creative pioneers, like those who settled in Monteverde, Costa Rica; though often the pioneering took place in science, engineering, business, or other professional work. A number became ministers of other denominations. Many became strong members of Friends meetings wherever they were, usually far from the old Conservative communities. Although many retained nonresident membership in their childhood meetings, very few actually founded new Conservative meetings. If they did help to found an unprogrammed meeting, it was usually independent, or it became attached to one of the regional groupings of Friends General Conference meetings.

In retrospect, we can see that much human energy for good was constantly being exported from the Conservative world throughout this century. We are glad for that contribution to wider Quakerism and wider Christianity, but sorry that the quietist and sometimes shy or introverted Conservative Friends were not able to maintain a more vital spiritual linkage with their brothers and sisters who served in the universities or worked in the great cities. Their contact with the complexities of the wider world might have brought back important insights and energy into the core Conservative community. There was plenty of energy and intelligence in the folk who remained in the rural core communities; some of them were also leaders in the secular communities and in the agricultural, business and professional world around them. However, it is somehow harder for those who stay in an old religious community to break out of the encrustations of group habit and adapt to new patterns of communication and organization.

As we approach the end of the century, one assessment of Conservative Friends might be that we are now rapidly losing the critical mass necessary for survival. This can be especially troubling to those who feel that we are in danger of losing our common sense of identity, our understanding of who we are and why we exist as a very small segment of the Religious Society of Friends. However, there are signs that even as the critical mass becomes smaller, there is a surprising increase of activity. For example, there is a movement toward Conservative Quakerism by individuals here and there in America and around the world who hunger for and are nourished by

Christ-centered waiting worship. Many of these people come with wide experience and a cosmopolitan background, so that their visits and membership can bring a breath of fresh air and encouragement to the older and sometimes discouraged meetings. Some of these new people as well as long-time members have also begun to revive the traveling ministry. They travel as far as England and Canada, especially to the Friends who hunger for the simplicity and depth of Christ-centered waiting worship. Here and there around the country little groups for Christ-centered waiting worship have begun to meet. Other examples of increased activity include more intervisitation and some increase in publications, as well as gatherings to better understand our roots or to consider a renewed concern for outreach and service.

Another sign of renewal is the way in which the traditional Queries are answered today in Ohio Yearly Meeting. They are no longer answered in the perfunctory wording that could be used (as in the days of Wilmer's youth); instead the answers are often long and painfully searching. In some meetings, different families or fellowship groups will take their turns in preparing a draft of the query answer, often spending considerable time searching for an honest account of our spiritual state in response to that month's query.

We agree with Wilmer's words in his closing chapter: "My plea is for them [Conservative Friends] to be themselves." Some of the increasing activity among Conservative Friends at this time comes from a recognition that, if we are to be true to who we are, we need to make the kind of study of our roots that Wilmer sets forth in Chapters 1 and 2. We have no choice in the face of our rapidly changing Conservative Quaker culture, which is bombarded by so many outside influences, but to intensify the search for our true identity and mission. Only if we know our true identity can we safely know how to adapt to the conditions of the modern world with integrity and faithfulness to our essential core. One thing is certain: change we must, or we will lose critical mass and soon become something that we are not.

1. From the days of George Fox until now, *Truth*, spelled with a capital T, has had a very special meaning for some groups of Friends. Its meaning included, of course, honesty and accuracy, but it meant much more that that. In its greatest breadth, it could even imply the entire greatness of God, and the way in which God has been and is at work through Christ, throughout all time. It also connotes that total way of life taught by Jesus. Therefore, to "know the Truth" or to "be in the Truth" would include being in living, breathing contact with Jesus the vine and teacher and guide, it would include living a life so stripped down and simplified (or "plain") that one would be available to "hear" or sense the slightest unexpected nudging from the Holy Spirit, and it would mean that one would be in spiritual invisible unity with those who know and have experienced inwardly the same invisible reality.

2. *Ohio Conservative Friends Review*, Summer,1996 (36:2). Book and Children's Literature Committee, Ohio Yearly Meeting of the Religious Society of Friends.

3. Samuel Cooper, *Memorial to Cyrus Cooper and Bertha A Cooper*. (Privately printed by Samuel Cooper), 1948, p. 33.

INTRODUCTION

W hen I finished my teaching and administrative career among Friends a few years ago, I felt that I wanted to reflect upon and write about my own early Conservative Friends upbringing, which has had a profound influence on my life. As you read the book you will note that I do not endorse all that Conservative Friends have espoused as the authentic Quaker/Christian way of life, but I do want to express my gratitude for much of the early training that was formative in my life. For this I owe a debt of gratitude to Conservative Wilburite Friends. At the same time I try to maintain a critical but appreciative attitude toward what I believe are their strengths and weaknesses.

Conservative Wilburite Friends have a very special place in the history of Friends in the nineteenth and twentieth centuries. They are relatively small in number and are less well known than some other branches of Friends. But there continues to be a sustained interest in who they are and where they fit into the Quaker jigsaw puzzle.

In this book I focus on a couple of facets of Conservative Quakerism. Although the book includes some history, its special emphasis is an autobiographical account of growing up among and being nurtured by Conservative Friends in the kind of Quaker conservatism that prevailed for a hundred years between 1850 to 1950. I have also taken the liberty of telling my own story beyond my early years because much of the nurturing and training I received in the Conservative Friends community has impacted my life and work in the wider Religious Society of Friends.

The second aspect of the book (see Chapter 2) is on the religious beliefs and faith commitments of Conservative Friends. Some might call this "Conservative Friends Faith and Practice." Here I have tried to do for Conservative Friends what my book, *A Living Faith: An Historical Study of Quaker Beliefs*, (1990) does for Friends in general.

Although Chapter 2 is an essential part of the book, some may find it difficult reading because it deals with the theological beliefs and religious practices of Conservative Friends for their first one hundred years. I encourage those who prefer to start with my personal pilgrimage to begin with Chapter 3. It is important to return later to the Quaker theological context in which I grew up, however, because my personal story can only be understood in the context of the historic faith and practice of Conservative Friends.

An important part of this book is the inclusion of a condensed version of John Brady's *A Short History of Conservative Friends* (1992) in Appendix C. Brady's study of Conservative Friends began in 1989 while he was studying Quakerism with Hugh Barbour and me at the Earlham School of Religion.

In addition to John Brady's historical treatment, I am also indebted to others who have in recent years helped to interpret Conservative Wilburite Friends. William Taber's *The Eye of Faith: A Short History of Ohio Yearly Meeting* (1985) provides a good account of the yearly meeting in which I grew up and which remains a stronghold of the Conservative Friends. Other shorter treatments of Conservative Friends include Charles P. Morlan, *A Brief History of Ohio Yearly Meeting of the Religious*

Society of Friends (Conservative), (1959), and Kenneth S. P. Morse, *A History of Conservative Friends*, (1962). For the history of Conservative Friends in North Carolina see Damon D. Hickey, *Sojourners No More: The Quakers in the New South 1865-1920*, (1997). Considering the historical roots of Conservative Friends before they became thus identified, I am intrigued by Kathryn Damiano's unpublished thesis entitled, "On Earth As It Is in Heaven: Eighteenth Century Quakerism As Realized Eschatology," 1988. She tries to capture the Quietistic mood and spirit of eighteenth-century Quakerism, which in turn was preserved and later lived out by Conservative Friends in the nineteenth and twentieth centuries. Also, I want to give credit to Thomas Hamm for his very thorough treatment in *The Transformation of American Quakerism: Orthodox Friends, 1800-1907*, (1988). This book provides the framework for understanding Quaker developments in the nineteenth century that gave rise to Conservative Friends. Hamm's book is must reading for anyone who tries to sort out and understand the Orthodox tradition of nineteenth century Quakerism. Only indirectly does it deal with the Hicksite liberal tradition, and only tangentially with Conservative Wilburite Friends.

I invite questions and further dialogue with any who wish to follow up on *Growing Up Plain*. None of us should ever conclude that we have said the last word, especially if we honor our Quaker belief in continuing revelation.

Wilmer A. Cooper
2030 Chester Boulevard, 16–B
Richmond, IN 47374

Chapter One

Conservative Friends Within the Quaker 'Mix'

Conservative Friends represent a stream of Quaker history that had its beginning in the seventeenth century and continued through the Quietistic period of Quakerism in the eighteenth century. I believe that Kathryn Damiano's doctoral thesis (1988) is right to challenge the usual interpretation of eighteenth-century Quakerdom as a low period of Friends history. Rather, she holds that Friends of the 1700s lived out in its purist form the authentic vision of George Fox and his followers in the seventeenth century.

Having grown up among Conservative Wilburite Friends, I am convinced that eighteenth-century Quaker Quietism was the spiritual forerunner of this tradition. And I also believe that the roots of Quaker Quietism go back to George Fox and the Quaker founders. The Religious Society of Friends—for Fox and the early founders, for Friends during the Quietistic period, and for Conservative Wilburite Friends in the nineteenth and early twentieth centuries—was primarily a spiritual movement committed to "waiting upon the Lord" with complete trust and confidence.

Conservative Friends were schooled in the writings of early Friends. I remember vividly my mother, Anna B. Cooper (1878-1954), reading devotionally the *Works of Isaac Penington.* I still possess the four volume set of Penington's works that nourished my mother's life. We were also familiar with George Fox's *Journal,* William Penn's *No Cross, No Crown,* and Robert Barclay's *Apology for the True Christian Divinity.* And these were always undergirded by the daily family reading of the Bible with a period of quiet worship and reflection following. As Kathryn Damiano would say, for these Friends, "life was lived from the 'inside out' rather than the 'outside in.'"

There are some Conservative Friends who wish there were a more accurate name to describe themselves. It is true that historically they intended to maintain and conserve the authentic character and tradition of the Religious Society of Friends. But to speak of them as "conservative" in the sense of being the opposite of liberal is misleading. This is especially true as applied to the name Conservative Friends today. It fits some Friends of this tradition, but not all. Historically they were conservative theologically and culturally, but there are Conservative Friends who might be considered progressive or even radical today. For want of a more accurate name the term will probably continue to be used.

The Conservative Friends yearly meetings took form in the nineteenth century following the Orthodox/Hicksite separations, which first occurred in Philadelphia, New York, and Ohio Yearly Meetings in 1827-28. These separations were social and cultural in origin but also reflected differing religious and theological perspectives.

In the late eighteenth and early nineteenth centuries, many Friends in England and America became increasingly conservative and evangelical in their understanding of religious authority and accountability. The followers of Elias Hicks (1748-1830), on the other hand, questioned the direction of this orthodoxy by emphasizing greater freedom of thought and the authority of the Light within as compared to the authority of Scripture and the Christian beliefs held by the Orthodox body. The conservative Orthodox position hardened, while the Hicksites pleaded for greater latitude in belief and practice. Also, the tenacity of certain strong leaders on both sides reduced the possibility of accommodation. Even today, after several generations, the divisions of 1827-28 have yet to be healed, although there is somewhat less tension and areas of cooperation are developing.

The Orthodox/Hicksite separation set the stage for still further discord and separations within the larger, Orthodox body itself. The chief name that came to be associated with the Orthodox branch was that of Joseph John Gurney (1788-1847), a prominent Friend from Norwich, England. He was a successful banker by profession and a recorded minister in London Yearly Meeting. He had important connections with prominent evangelical Christians in England, who many believe influenced his Quaker beliefs in ways that conflict with historic Quakerism.

The other chief figure in this second round of separations was John Wilbur (1774-1856), a recorded minister from South Kingston Meeting in New England Yearly Meeting. He lived at Hopkinton, Rhode Island, where he received his general education and later became a school teacher. He was also a farmer and surveyor. He was appointed an elder in his meeting at age 28, and ten years later (1812) he was recorded as a minister of the Gospel. John Wilbur claimed the infallibility of the Inward Teacher, who was made known by the Holy Spirit and the Light of Christ within. Wilbur and his followers mistrusted the rational faculties of our human nature, which for them constituted "creaturely activity" that often disregarded the inward leading of the Holy Spirit.

During the years 1831-33 Wilbur visited Friends in England and Ireland. He was acceptable to that minority of British Friends who were steeped in *Barclay's Apology*, and who wanted to maintain the Quietistic traditions of "ancient Friends." During a visit to Norwich, the home of Joseph John Gurney, he asked for an "appointed meeting," but when it was held, he felt that his message was not heard because the meeting was dominated by Gurney's supporters. During this same stay in England, John Wilbur wrote a series of seven letters to George Crosfield, which were later published under the title *Letters to a Friend on Some of the Primitive Doctrines of Christianity* (1832). These letters dealt with a variety of doctrinal matters, including the place of the atonement and the authority of Scripture in Quaker thought. The last letter took up matters of "plainness and self-denial." The central message was to preserve the past and maintain the "hedge" mentality of eighteenth-century Quietism, which was meant to protect members from the "evil" influences of the outside world.

Back in New England, Wilbur continued to attack Gurney, who by now was accepted as an "approved minister" among the Orthodox Friends in America. Wilbur's persistence finally split New England Yearly Meeting into the "Larger Body" (Gurney Orthodox) and the "Smaller Body" (Wilburite Conservative) in 1845. Leading up to this separation, disciplinary action was taken against Wilbur when his Rhode Island Quarterly Meeting asked that his South Kingston Monthly Meeting disown him because of his stand against Gurney. When it refused, the quarterly meeting laid down South Kingston Meeting and transferred the monthly meeting's membership to Greenwich Monthly Meeting; Greenwich Monthly Meeting took action in 1843 to disown John Wilbur from the Religious Society of Friends. Wilbur made an appeal to the yearly meeting to rescind the action of Greenwich Monthly Meeting, but he received no response. At that point about 500 of Wilbur's supporters (10 percent of the yearly meeting) withdrew and formed New England Yearly Meeting (Conservative).

A similar but larger split took place in Ohio Yearly Meeting in 1854 between the "Hoyle" Conservatives and the "Binns" Gurneyites, who took their names from their respective clerks. In the meantime, Philadelphia Arch Street Yearly Meeting (Orthodox) tended to side with John Wilbur against Gurney, except for Twelfth Street Meeting and Haverford College. Philadelphia temporarily resolved its dilemma of who to recognize by discontinuing its annual epistles to other yearly meetings. In 1924 it resumed sending general epistles to all yearly meetings.

For the next quarter of a century Conservative separations from Orthodox Gurney branches of Friends continued. Basically there were two streams of separations; the first included New England in 1845 and Ohio in 1854. During this same period, there were minor separations in isolated monthly and quarterly meetings, such as Nottingham Meeting in Baltimore Yearly Meeting and Scipio Quarter in New York Yearly Meeting. Some of these were called "Primitive Friends," but they were too few in number to threaten yearly meeting-wide divisions. These early separatists at mid-century claimed to be "faithful remnants" holding to the "ancient truths and testimonies" of early Friends as articulated by Robert Barclay and John Wilbur. They stood for plainness of speech and dress and were committed to self denial in their manner of living. They opted for self-imposed isolation from the world and chose not to proselytize others, which may account for their lack of growth in subsequent years.

A second stream of Conservative Friends separated from their yearly meetings not so much out of loyalty to the tradition of Barclay and Wilbur, but because they were opposed to the inroads of emotional revivalism encouraged by traveling evangelists through the Midwest, and to a lesser degree in the South. This mode of Christian expression was primarily the result of the Second Great Awakening of evangelicals (influenced by John Wesley and Charles Finney), who impacted communities where Friends resided in Indiana, Iowa, Kansas and North Carolina. The discomfort with the appearance of emotional revivalism among some Friends resulted in Conservative separations in Western (Indiana) Yearly Meeting (1877), Iowa Yearly Meeting (1877), Kansas Yearly Meeting (1879), and Canada Yearly Meeting (1881). Somewhat later in 1904, a segment of North Carolina conservatively minded Friends separated from the main body of North Carolina Yearly Meeting. This was primarily over the adoption of a Uniform Discipline intended to govern the Gurney Orthodox yearly meetings affiliated with the newly formed Five Years Meeting of Friends in 1902, with headquarters in Richmond, Indiana.

Thus, by the turn of the century, Conservative Friends had formed seven yearly meetings spread across the country from Kansas to the East Coast, to the north into Canada, and as far south as North Carolina. They also had close ties with Philadelphia Arch Street Yearly Meeting (Orthodox). Conservative Friends were largely a reaction to Gurneyite Quakerism and have been described by Damon Hickey as a "counter culture" of Friends and by William Taber as a Friends "subculture." They chose to live out the earlier Quaker reputation of a "peculiar people" determined to "bear the cross of plainness" (Damon Hickey) and produce the fruits of "primitive Christianity revived" (William Penn).

Traditional Quakerism was a religious culture, not just a set of doctrines and liturgies, a mutually-reinforcing blend of theology and rigorous disciplines that affected nearly every area of life and set Quakers apart as "a peculiar people." The outward signs of difference were borne by Friends as a "cross," a burdensome testimony to the world of their beliefs and commitments. The plainness and simplicity of Quaker worship without music, [prepared] sermons, formal prayers, or religious symbols, were expressions of Quaker inwardness, the effort to maintain an inner stillness and receptiveness to divine leading. And so Quaker culture took on the aspect of both subculture and counterculture. As a subculture it sought to preserve distinctive ways in order to define its separation from the larger society. As a counterculture it sought from the beginning to overcome the ways of the world and to witness to a revolutionary system of values.[1]

Wilburite Friends shared many of the same Christian beliefs held by Gurneyite Friends, who in turn had been influenced by evangelical Christianity. Both Wilbur and Gurney were Christ-centered in their faith. They shared a belief in the virgin birth and the divine/human nature of Jesus Christ—a doctrine often referred to as the divinity of Christ, which places less emphasis on the humanity of Jesus. They shared a view of Christ's sacrificial death on the cross as being critical for salvation. And they shared a belief in the New Testament passion account of Jesus' death and resurrection. Gurney and Wilbur were both orthodox in the sense that they opposed Elias Hicks and the liberal tradition Hicks came to symbolize in nineteenth-century Quakerism.

There were two major theological differences between Wilbur and Gurney. The first concerned their respective views of the source of religious authority. Even though both took the

Bible seriously and believed in the Divine inspiration of Scripture, they differed over whether Scripture itself or the Holy Spirit that gave forth Scripture was the primary authority. Wilburite Friends believed revelation is not closed with the Bible but continues through the gift of the Holy Spirit, available to all faithful followers of the Living Christ within. Although the Wilburites were well grounded in the Scriptures they did not believe in "studying" the Bible as an intellectual pursuit. The Scriptures could only be understood in the same Spirit that gave them forth and were not a subject to be taught in the classroom.

The second theological difference between Wilbur and Gurney was their view of justification by faith, a traditional Protestant doctrine of salvation. Gurney placed primary emphasis on the sacrificial death of Jesus on the cross as necessary and sufficient for salvation. Upon acknowledgment of this article of faith, one could then expect to grow in grace and become sanctified before God. Wilbur, although he accepted the necessity of Christ's atonement for sin, believed none are justified apart from obedience to Christ in daily life. Thus Wilburites held to the traditional Quaker belief that Christ's righteousness cannot be imputed to the individual believer; rather, it is the responsibility of each believer to become perfected in the school of Christ. Unless this takes place we simply condone the continuation of sin in our lives.

Besides these two major theological differences between Wilbur and Gurney, there were other aspects of faith and practice which plagued their relationship. Because of their view of Scripture and the necessity of its interpretation by the Holy Spirit, Wilburite Friends did not approve of First Day Schools, where the Bible was studied and truths derived therefrom were taught. Moreover, Wilburites objected to Friends adopting the Sunday School movement, which had become so prevalent among other churches by mid-century.

Because of the Conservative's utter belief in reliance upon the Holy Spirit, they did not believe Friends should prepare advanced messages for meeting for worship; rather they were to respond to the immediate inspiration and guidance of the Spirit of Christ in worship and spoken ministry. In like manner they declined, for the most part, to follow many other churches who were increasingly caught up in the foreign missionary movement. This seems surprising, since George Fox and a multitude of early Friends had traveled the world over to carry the Gospel message to other lands and peoples.

In fairness to Joseph John Gurney, many of the differences between Wilburite Friends and Gurneyite Friends did not become accentuated for another twenty-five years or more after his death in 1846. During Gurney's lifetime Friends in England still maintained the quiet meeting where they "waited upon the Lord" in worship and for ministry. It was after the death of Gurney and Wilbur that Orthodox Gurneyite Friends in America adopted the "pastoral system" of worship and ministry, which included prepared sermons and prayers, music and hymn singing, testimonial meetings, and emotional revival meetings with altar calls and instant conversions. Many Conservative Friends, however, believed that the roots of these later developments were inherent in the teachings of Joseph John Gurney, and therefore they were opposed by Wilbur's followers.

One can see now why John Wilbur became unalterably opposed to what he believed to be Gurney's departure from the "ancient truths and testimonies" of Friends as set forth in Robert Barclay's *Apology*. Wilbur was devoted to guarding the old ways and maintaining "the hedge" around the religious society which Conservative Friends had adopted from the quietistic Quaker tradition of the eighteenth century.

Today Conservative Friends represent a small and declining number of Friends with an uncertain future. At the same time, they maintain a standard of Quakerism handed down from the past that is admired, respected, and coveted by many in the Religious Society of Friends who have departed from some of the norms set by George Fox and his followers. Out of the seven Conservative Yearly Meetings only three remain: Ohio, North Carolina, and Iowa, which have a combined membership of around 1,500. Each of the three have gained a few new meetings that have been formed out of worship groups geographically adjacent to their respective yearly meetings.

Damon Hickey makes an important observation, which could apply not only to North Carolina Yearly Meeting (Conservative), but also to Iowa Yearly Meeting (Conservative), and to a lesser degree to Ohio Yearly Meeting (Conservative). Referring to new urban meetings or worship groups that joined North Carolina Yearly Meeting Hickey comments:

> Although unprogrammed and without pastors, they were far more intellectual, cosmopolitan, theologically diverse, and "worldly," than the old Friends from Southern Quarter would have wished. The numbers were finally increasing, but not for the reason they had expected.[2]

Conservative Friends have maintained or are involved with four Friends schools: Olney Friends Boarding School at Barnesville, Ohio; Scattergood Friends School at West Branch, Iowa; Carolina Friends School at Durham, North Carolina; and Virginia Beach Friends School in Virginia Beach, Virginia. All of the original one-room elementary schoolhouses maintained by Conservative Friends have been laid down, but a few new Friends elementary schools have sprung up that are partially supported and maintained by Conservative Friends.

1. Damon Hickey, *Sojourners No More: The Quakers in the New South, 1865-1920* (Greensboro, NC: North Carolina Friends Historical Society), 1997, p. 79.

2. Damon Hickey, "Bearing the Cross of Plainess: Conservative Quaker Culture in North Carolina" (unpublished M. A. thesis, University of North Carolina at Greensboro, 1982) p. 82.

Chapter Two

Conservative Friends Faith Commitments

Even though Friends have been prolific writers throughout their history, devotional literature was common and their journals were a living record of God's dealing with them in public ministry and service. In addition to journal writing Friends have written extensively about their own history. Since Quakers did not have a formal creed to establish their identity, they wrote Quaker history by telling and retelling their story in order to establish their identity and keep alive the tradition. Telling their story was probably the Quaker equivalent to repeating the creeds in the other churches. Friends also had religious and social testimonies as an outward expression of their inward spiritual leadings, which was another way of establishing their identity.

Friends have seldom produced theological writings that systematically articulate their doctrines and religious beliefs. Robert Barclay's *Apology*, written within the first twenty-five years of the Religious Society of Friends (in which he set forth a systematic interpretation of their faith and practice) was an exception. My book, *A Living Faith: An Historical Study of Quaker Beliefs* (1990), is, in its own way, also a systematic interpretation of Quaker beliefs.

George Fox, as founder of the Religious Society of Friends, was not primarily concerned with theological belief. For him the most important question was: "What canst thou say" with respect to the "workings of God and of Christ in thy life?"

Although the *experience* of God and of Christ is primary for Friends, this tenet also presupposes *belief* in God and the inward Christ, and the presence of the Holy Spirit to transmit that experience. To become practitioners of our faith and religious experience, we have to reflect upon and interpret it with our rational faculties, at which point we are, in fact, theologizing.

Even though many Friends disparage theology and claim that "belief" is either to be denied or is unimportant, the fact is we all have basic beliefs and commitments pertaining to our religious faith and practice.

Conservative Friends have given expression to a fairly consistent pattern of religious beliefs and practices that were rooted in the Bible and Christian faith as interpreted by George Fox and other early Friends. The Bible was of course basic for all early Friends, as it was for Conservatives. Some said that if the Scriptures were lost, Fox could rewrite them from memory—a claim that may seem a little suspect. Other major writings for Conservative Friends were George Fox's *Journal*, William Penn's *No Cross, No Crown*, and the *Works of Isaac Penington*. But doubtless the most important of all was Robert Barclay's *Apology*. This became the benchmark for testing the orthodoxy of Conservative Wilburite Quakerism for a century or more. And of course there were also the journals of many

Friends ministers through the years which were cited and read by Conservative Friends, especially John Woolman's *Journal* (1769).

Later there was the *Journal of the Life of John Wilbur: A Minister of the Gospel in the Society of Friends* (1859) and *The Letters of John Wilbur to George Crosfield* (1879). The latter was originally written in England when Wilbur was on a religious visit among Friends in England from 1831-1833.

The nineteenth-century historian of Conservative Friends was William Hodgson. He wrote *The Society of Friends in the Nineteenth Century* (1875) and *The Society of Friends in the Nineteenth Century: A Historical View of Successive Convulsions and Schisms Therein During that Period* (two volumes 1875 and 1876). Although of historical significance, these two volumes are sometimes lacking in objectivity. They tend to consider other branches of Friends with disfavor, if not disdain. Some of the same criticisms were made earlier by John Wilbur himself. And, unfortunately, similar judgments were made of the Conservatives by their adversaries from the other side.

Two other important publications that help us to evaluate and gain an understanding of Conservative Friends appeared in the early part of the twentieth century. The first was a collection of essays by Philadelphia Yearly Meeting (the Orthodox Arch Street branch), which sympathized with Conservative Friends but never officially identified with them. This valuable book was entitled *Principles of Quakerism* (1909). The other was entitled *A Brief Synopsis of the Principles and Testimonies of the Religious Society of Friends* (1913), hereafter referred to as *Brief Synopsis*. When this document was adopted the year before its publication in 1913, it was endorsed by all seven Conservative yearly meetings and circulated for their use. It includes the seven letters of approval from the Conservative yearly meetings.

These two publications, together with Robert Barclay's *Apology*, give us the clearest summary of Friends faith and practice among non-Gurneyite Orthodox Quakers at the turn of the twentieth century, especially those identified as Conservative Wilburite Friends. Of course, the larger body of Orthodox Friends (as compared with the Hicksite branch, now Friends General Conference) were those belonging to the Gurneyite tradition, which was made up of mostly pastoral Friends meetings of the Five Years Meeting (now Friends United Meeting, with headquarters in Richmond, Indiana). Later, another branch of pastoral Friends formed the Evangelical Friends Alliance (now renamed Evangelical Friends International).

What Was the Faith and Practice of Conservative Friends ?

The beginning of the Conservative Friends statement of 1913 cited above boldly set forth their faith, quoting primarily from George Fox's *Journal*. The second half of this quotation from Fox is a verbatim re-statement of his famous Letter to the Governor of Barbadoes.

> Real Friends today believe, as did George Fox, in the one only wise, omnipotent, omniscient, omnipresent and eternal God, "The Creator of all things, in heaven and in earth, and the preserver of all that He has made, who is God over all, blessed forever; to whom be all honor, glory, dominion, praise and thanksgiving, both now, henceforth and forever more. And we own and believe in Jesus Christ, His beloved and only begotten Son, in whom He is well pleased; who was conceived by the Holy Ghost, and born of the virgin Mary; in whom we have redemption through His blood, even the forgiveness of sins; who is the express image of the invisible

God, by whom were all things created that are in heaven and in earth, visible, and invisible."[1]

When the statement refers to "real Friends," we may assume it not only acknowledges what George Fox believed, but also describes what Conservative Wilburite Friends believed. The statement continues: "We...affirm our belief in His [i.e. Christ's] atoning sacrifice on Calvary, for the sins of all mankind....We are led to repent of, and forsake our sins, so through the atoning efficacy of the blood of Christ...we are enabled to experience remission of our past sins." It is important to note the words "past sins." Conservative Friends then clinch this belief with a statement from Robert Barclay: "We believe that the remission of sins, which any partake of, is only in, and by virtue of that most satisfactory sacrifice, and no[t] otherwise"[2]

John Wilbur in his *Letters to George Crosfield* affirms his belief in the centrality of Jesus Christ and his commitment to belief in the atoning work of Christ's death.

> If any man with the Bible in his hand, shall deny the divinity of Christ, and the efficacy and necessity of his outward sacrifice, then all his professions of light or grace, or spirit...will be but a mere...counterfeit...and will only contribute to his condemnation.[3]

John Wilbur further declares that "the plan of salvation and redemption" consists of 1) repentance, 2) the atoning blood of Christ, and 3) the Holy Spirit which sanctifies.[4] He criticizes the Socinians (i.e. Unitarians) and the Hicksite Friends for stress on "the light! the light! the spirit!...and Christ within but *not without!*" And he links the Socinians and Hicksites together for denying the divinity and atonement of Christ.[5]

These statements of faith may seem doctrinaire and more like the early creeds of the churches that Friends have felt uncomfortable with or have rejected. Although that may be true, it is instructive that Philadelphia Yearly Meeting (Arch Street before uniting with Race Street in 1955) states the following:

> The early Friends…preached 'primitive Christianity revived.' Their central doctrine, a doctrine which they felt had been lost sight of in the course of centuries, was that of the Universal and Saving Light of Christ in the hearts of all men. [But] they had also full belief in the inspiration of scripture, and the Deity of Christ and the atonement made by Him for the sins of the whole world.[6]

The statement of faith by George Fox quoted above sounds Trinitarian, whereas Friends in general denied the doctrine of the Trinity as unbiblical, in that it emphasized the threeness rather than the oneness of the Godhead. The 1913 *Brief Synopsis* makes this qualified and clarifying Trinitarian statement:

> Friends believe in the "Three who bear record in heaven, Father, Son and Holy Ghost," and that these are one; yet we have ever been concerned to avoid the word "Trinity" as applied to the Divine Being as not found in the Bible…and more confusing than the Plain and simple terms used in the Scriptures. [Quoting Thomas Evans] "We avoid entangling ourselves by the use of unscriptural terms, invented to define Him who is undefinable, scrupulously adhering to the safe and simple language as contained in the Holy Scriptures."[7]

Scripture

Following the counsel of Robert Barclay, Conservative Friends have affirmed the authority of Scripture and its place in their faith and practice. In *Brief Synopsis* they say:

> In common with other orthodox and evangelical bodies, we
> accept, and believe in the authenticity, and Divine authority
> of the Holy Scriptures, and would quote from Robert Bar-
> clay: "Yet we may not call them the principal fountain of all
> truth and knowledge, nor yet the first adequate rule of faith
> and manners, because the principal fountain of truth must be
> the truth itself."[8]

The source of "the truth itself" for Barclay was the Spirit
of God who inspired and gave forth the Scriptures. This same
Spirit is the fountainhead from which all truth and knowledge
flow.[9] Here Barclay quotes 2 Timothy 3:16, "all Scripture is
inspired by God and profitable for teaching, for reproof, for
correction, and for training in righteousness...."[10] Therefore,
writes Barclay, "we consider them the only proper outward judge
of controversy among Christians."[11]

Conservatives, like other Friends, do not believe that the
Bible is the "Word of God," but rather the "words of God."
They hold that the "Word" referred to in the Gospel of John
1:1 is the *Logos* (in Greek) and refers to Christ: "In the beginning was the Word, and the Word was with God, and the Word
was God." No lesser theologian of the twentieth century than
Karl Barth has written volumes on Christ as the Word (*Logos*)
of God. This is a Biblical understanding that Friends have
claimed from their beginning years.

But one should not conclude from this that Conservative
Friends have placed much confidence in Biblical scholarship
to discern the leading of the Spirit. In fact, *Brief Synopsis* states:

> "Neither would we have any think that our attitude toward
> the Holy Scriptures...is induced by any leaning toward or
> sympathy for that refined species of unbelief, known as 'Higher
> Criticism'...." They have claimed that this approach to the

Scriptures calls into question many things recorded in the Bible and thereby "has shaken the faith of many an honest inquirer after the Truth."[12]

As we enumerate further other items of faith and practice according to Conservative Friends, we will find that historically they used Scripture extensively both to claim and disclaim their theological beliefs. They not only measured the inner truth claims against a literal reading of the Scriptures, but they knew them so well that in ministry and journal writing they quoted Scripture liberally as "proof" for what they felt led by the Spirit of God to proclaim.

One of the pitfalls of Conservative Friends, and many conservative Christians, is to insist on a literal interpretation of Scripture. This often distorts the true and deeper meaning. There are other modes of speaking and writing besides literal discourse. There are poetry, allegory, myth, and the use of various figures of speech: simile, metaphor and hyperbole, to mention a few. Conservative Friends have not been accustomed to using imagination or various art forms to communicate the meaning of reality and truth. This is probably the reason they used to denounce and forbid fiction, fairy tales, and stories that they believed fantasized truth and reality. I know all of this firsthand from my strict Conservative Friends upbringing. To not be conversant with other modes of communication has been a handicap for me and it is part of my early Conservative Wilburite training that I regret.

The Resurrection

The early Friends view of the nature and work of Christ was premised on the truth and reality of the Resurrection. Conser-

vative Friends minced no words in affirming the Christian belief
that either Christ's resurrection following the crucifixion really happened or Jesus was a fraud. *Brief Synopsis* states: "We
fully accept and believe in the resurrection of the dead as taught
by Christ and the Apostles." It cites, especially, Paul in I
Corinthians 15:

> With him we believe in the resurrection, not of the body, but
> of the spirit.... God giveth it a body as it hath pleased Him
> and to every seed his own body.... It is sown in corruption, it
> is raised in incorruption; it is sown in dishonor, it is raised in
> glory: it is sown in weakness, it is raised in power; it is sown a
> natural body, it is raised a spiritual body. There is a natural
> body, and there is a spiritual body.[13]

Worship

Having affirmed the reality of God and the power of the res-
urrected living Christ, Friends from the beginning felt con-
strained to make public confession of this and gather regularly
for the purpose of Divine worship. They drew their pattern of
worship from the Gospel of John 4:24: "God is spirit, and they
that worship Him must worship Him in spirit and in truth."
To quote again from the Conservative Friends document:
"...We endeavor, when thus assembled, to attain a condition
of quiet introversion of mind, waiting upon the Lord, with all
our expectation directed unto Him, the great Head of the
Church...."[14]

 Friends did not refer so much to "worship" as they did to
"waiting upon the Lord." This waiting "...is not a vacant or
listless waiting, but is 'an intense activity of soul,' a true 'exercise of spirit.' It is not properly waiting *for* the Lord to come to

us, but waiting *in* his presence, intently watching for his directing hand and call."[15] One of the most moving statements about Friends worship was made by Robert Barclay following his first visit to a Friends meeting:

> For when I came into the silent assemblies of God's people, I felt a secret power among them, which touched my heart. And as I gave way to it, I found the evil in me weakening, and the good lifted up. Thus it was that I was knit into them and united with them. And I hungered more for the increase of this power and life until I could feel myself perfectly redeemed.[16]

Not until the middle of the nineteenth century, with the appearance of the pastoral/programmed meetings, did music become a part of Friends worship. Philadelphia Yearly Meeting's (Arch Street) *Principles of Quakerism* states forthrightly the historic objection of Friends to music:

> It has been observed…that the emotions produced by music, exalted though they may be, are not to be confused with the pure motions of the Divine Spirit, which arise in the quiet of the soul. These breathe forth at times with a heavenly sweetness that no music among men can equal, and when once known, are preferred to all outward harmonies, being…the harmony of heaven itself.[17]

The question may be asked whether single performers may not truly act under the prompting of the Spirit in the rendering of hymns, just as ministers speak and recite passages of Scripture.

> …[Although] singing is mentioned on rare occasions among the early Friends…. [It is] in practice felt to be inexpedient in

Friends' worship, and out of harmony with the prophetic type ministry.[18]

Friends believed there can be an inward spiritual harmony and melody of the heart that is in tune with the Spirit of God, which surpasses the understanding of the mind.

Ministry

Friends historically had a prophetic understanding of ministry in the context of worship. This is not the kind of prophecy that foretells the future, but rather one that proclaims "the word of the Lord." Ministry was prompted and informed by the Holy Spirit, and anyone who was not attuned to that same Spirit was not regarded as able to deliver a message from the Lord.

Friends also had a testimony against the "paid ministry," which some pastoral Friends today have dubbed the "poorly paid ministry!" There was always the fear that remuneration for ministry would make the minister beholden to one's hearers, so as to compromise the proclamation of the Gospel truth. It seemed to Friends to be contrary to the prophetic ministry which is "freely received" and, therefore, should be "freely given."

Another bothersome matter was whether a minister of the Gospel should have special preparation or training for ministry. The Conservative Friends statement of 1913 says:

> There is a subtle influence at work in many places… to exalt an intellectual, or educational standard for the ministry….We do not wish to discourage, in the least, a liberal and thorough education; but we would raise a warning voice against making the ministry of the gospel of Christ, at all dependent upon

a college education, or intellectual attainment....We believe it is of great advantage to ministers frequently to read the Holy Scriptures, having their minds turned to the Spirit, by which they were dictated, and which alone can open the Divine mysteries contained in them.[19]

[The Philadelphia Arch Street statement reads]: The Society of Friends, while valuing intellectual attainment, and taking a leading part in education, does not believe that its ministers should be set apart for a special education to fit them to preach the Gospel. The reason for this lies in the fact that they desire to preserve a ministry of the prophetic type.... A first hand experience of the things of God is the chief preparation; habitual living in communion with Him; receiving the messages and inspiration of his Spirit.... The living gospel is essentially a spiritual thing, not a dogma of theology; it is rather a vital force, to be received fresh and strong from God, more by the heart than the head.... On the other hand it is recognized that the intellect has its right place; and that a measure of intellectual processes must enter ministry....[20]

Friends do not ordain for ministry "by laying on of hands" to consecrate the minister in the "apostolic succession." Rather, they record persons gifted in ministry by the Holy Spirit.

When a person has frequently spoken acceptably in meeting for worship, and those of discernment believe that this speaking indicates the bestowal of a real spiritual gift from God, that gift, with concurrence of the congregation, is simply acknowledged to exist, by recording him [or her] as a minister.[21]

The Sacraments

One of the most debated issues between Friends and other Christians has been the sacraments of the Church in worship.

In Robert Barclay's *Apology*, two of his Propositions (equivalent to chapters) are devoted to the sacraments of Baptism and the Lord's Supper. The avowed purpose of a sacrament (especially the Lord's Supper) is to remember, celebrate and re-enact the life, death and resurrection of Jesus Christ. Some Christians refer to the sacraments as "ordinances" because they believe they were ordained by Jesus. The Roman Catholic Church celebrates seven sacraments, whereas the Protestant Reformation reduced the essential sacraments (or ordinances) to two— Baptism and the Lord's Supper. Because Friends arose in England a century following the Protestant Reformation, and because they sprang in part from the radical left wing of Protestantism, we need to look carefully at the contrasting positions held by different Friends.

Conservative Friends have agreed with the historic Quaker opposition to the outward forms of the sacraments, or ordinances. This is one place where most Friends, including the Conservative Wilburites, have found themselves on common ground with other branches of Friends. Because Friends were born out of the movement of the Spirit in their personal and corporate lives, they rejected symbolism, outward forms, ceremonies, and rites that they believed belonged to the old Jewish covenant. Jesus, they believed, came to initiate a new covenant rooted in the direct and immediate presence of God in their midst.

Early Friends found nothing in the New Testament that made water baptism mandatory. Friends have always believed in baptism by the Holy Spirit as necessary to enter into a new relationship with God through Christ; therefore it is incorrect to say that Friends do not believe in baptism. But the cleansing from sin and entrance into new life of faith is through the Spirit and not with the use of water, regardless of how the ceremony is performed.

Historically Friends quoted Scripture to support their position. Ephesians 4:5 speaks of "one Lord, one faith and one baptism," while Matthew 3:11 quotes John the Baptist: "I baptize you with water for repentance, but he who is coming after me [referring to Jesus] will baptize you with the Holy Spirit and fire." Many cite Jesus' admonition in Matthew 28:19: "Go therefore and make disciples of all nations, baptizing them in the name of the Father and of the Son and of the Holy Spirit." But Friends point out that the passage makes no mention of "water baptism" as such.

Friends give the sacrament of the Lord's Supper a spiritual interpretation. A Scriptural reference frequently quoted by early Friends was Revelations 3:20: "Behold, I stand at the door and knock; if any one hears my voice and opens the door, I will come in to him and eat with him, and he with me." Friends would like every meal and every meeting for worship to be a time of holy communion in the presence of the Lord. Conservative Friends further state:

> With these spiritual views of the religion of Christ, it would be inconsistent for Friends to believe in the ritual of the Eucharist.... Our contention is that our Lord did not, by eating of the Passover with his disciples, institute any new rite, or ordinance, but was observing with them, the last act in the Mosaic law, which was fulfilled and abrogated by our Savior's most acceptable sacrifice of Himself....[22]

Friends point out that if Jesus had intended the Last Supper to be enshrined as a command to his followers, why then does the Gospel of John substitute the command of foot washing at the same place where the Gospels of Matthew, Mark and Luke record the sharing of the loaf and the cup at the last meal Jesus had with his disciples? Canby Jones, a student of George Fox, writes:

[Fox] actually believed in only one Sacrament, that of being grafted into Christ....Though he speaks of both baptism and the Lord's Supper, he spiritualizes them into essentially the same thing....Now that Christ the substance has come all types and shadows of him are of no more use.[23]

The Quaker Testimonies

The Quaker testimonies have been referred to in various ways and under different names. For a fuller treatment of the subject, read *A Living Faith* (1990), Chapter 8. There I make a differentiation between the "religious testimonies" and the "social testimonies" of Friends. Hopefully Friends will never claim a discontinuity between the two, but for descriptive purposes the distinction may be helpful. Friends views of the Light within (or the Light of Christ within, as early Friends almost always said), or Friends views of worship and ministry, or their views on Baptism and the Lord's Supper, can be thought of as "religious testimonies." But Friends concern about war and peace, truth-telling and integrity, simple lifestyle, and the equality of all before God are usually referred to as "social testimonies."

A defining statement about the meaning of testimonies needs to be made at the start:

A testimony is an outward expression of an inward leading of the Spirit, or an outward sign of what Friends believe to be an inward revelation of truth....The testimonies provide the moral and ethical fruits of one's inward life of the Spirit. To quote Worth Hartman, "They arise more out of a concern for purity, holiness, consistency with divine order than from a passion for social justice." In a very real sense the testimonies are the Quaker "articles of faith" translated into action.[24]

There is also an important connection between the testimonies and the sacraments for Friends. Since Augustine's time in the fourth century, the Church has defined a sacrament as a "visible sign of invisible reality." This means that it is something sacred, holy, and majestic in relationship to God. In this sense Friends speak sacramentally when they say that not just the Lord's Supper but every meal should be a sacramental meal, and every meeting for worship should be a time of holy communion with God—not just those times when the bread and the wine are shared as an act of worship.

So in a sense, every outward testimony of Friends has a sacramental source and quality because it is grounded in God and arises when we feel led to give outward expression to our inner promptings of the Spirit. Although Conservative Friends have not normally spoken of the sacraments/ordinanaces and the social testimonies in this sense, I believe that it is this very grounding in God and our response to the inner promptings of the Spirit to which we refer when we speak of the Biblical basis for the Quaker view of the sacraments and testimonies.

Integrity

Perhaps basic to all the Friends testimonies is the Testimony of Integrity. This testimony was exemplified in their respect for the truth, taking the form of truth-telling, coupled with a commitment to honesty, in all of their dealings. (Friends were called "Friends of the Truth" and "Children of the Light" before they became known as the Religious Society of Friends.)

The Testimony of Integrity was reflected most clearly and used most frequently among early Friends when they were brought before magistrates and refused to testify under oath that they would "now" tell the truth. Friends wanted to be known for telling the truth all the time and not just when they were placed under oath. Their first stated reason for refusing to take the oath was that followers of Christ were forbidden by Scripture from swearing under oath. They relied on two New Testament passages in support of this particular testimony:

> Again ye have heard that it hath been said by them of old time, Thou shalt not forswear thyself [that is, swear falsely], but shalt perform unto the Lord thine oaths. But I say unto you, Swear not at all; neither by heaven; for it is God's throne; nor by the earth, for it is his footstool; neither by Jerusalem; for it is the city of the great King. Neither shalt thou swear by thy head; because thou canst not make one hair white or black. But let your communication be Yea, yea; Nay, nay; for whatsoever is more than these cometh of evil. (Matt. 5:33-37)

James clearly prohibits swearing:

> But, above all things, my brethren, swear not, neither by heaven, neither by the earth, neither by any other oath; but let your yea be yea; and your nay, nay; lest you fall into condemnation." (James 5:12)

In 1689, the Act of Toleration gave Friends in England significant concessions in their struggle for religious liberty. But it was not until 1722 that Friends were allowed to substitute a simple affirmation in place of a formal oath. This helped them to maintain their single standard of truth as a living testimony to "the world's people."

Peace

The issues of war and violence (or "fighting" as Barclay would say) and the question of how to settle differences in a peaceful way are the concerns of the Friends Peace Testimony. This is probably the best known Quaker testimony. Here Friends agree with the other Historic Peace Churches: the Mennonites and the Church of the Brethren. The 1913 *Synopsis* states:

> The whole trend of the Savior's teaching is in opposition to all war!! What could be more comprehensive in its scope, what more definite than his words as recorded in Matt. 5:43-45:

> "Ye have heard that it hath been said, 'Thou shalt love thy neighbor, and hate thine enemy.' But I say unto you, love your enemies, bless them that curse you, do good to them that hate you, and pray for them which despitefully use you and persecute you that ye may be the children of your Father which is in heaven...." Certainly we can imagine nothing more at variance with the gospel plan, than the hatred and violence of war!! [25]

Friends have given other than Biblical reasons for opposing war and violence. The following is an example of a moral argument recorded by Philadelphia Yearly Meeting (Arch Street):

> We cannot fight for we believe that fighting itself is immoral and we will not do wrong even for a righteous cause. If there is no other alternative we can suffer, as we have shown our capacity to suffer...and conquered by [*sic*] suffering. [26]

Simplicity

The Friends Testimony of Simplicity is a very important standard for life and behavior, which historically has been expressed in a variety of ways reaching beyond the meaning often associated with it today. Whereas we tend to think of it as an unencumbered and simplified style of dress and outward behavior, earlier Friends avoided ornamentation in the furnishing of their homes, schools, and places of business, as well as in dress. Historically, Friends certainly carried simplicity farther than do most Friends today, referring to the days of the week and the months of the year numerically rather than naming them after pagan idols and gods (i.e. First Day [Sunday], Fifth Day [Thursday], Ninth Month [September]).

For early Friends, living out a Testimony of Simplicity held meanings that now are included within the Quaker Testimony of Equality. For example, Friends concern for simplicity of speech carried a connotation of equality. In the seventeenth century ecclesiastical and magisterial authorities expected their subjects to address them in the plural "You," or "Your Honor." "Thus originated the plural form of speech, to one person, which has now become well nigh universal...." Also, Fox and his followers refused to use complimentary titles and terms in addressing persons of a different rank.[27]

The Quaker practice of truth-telling and concern for integrity have also sometimes been subsumed under the Testimony of Simplicity. Probably the reason was a concern to avoid duplicity (i.e. a double standard) rather than the simplicity of a single standard of truth-telling. The Scriptural admonition that undergirds this avoidance of duplicity is found in the King James version of Matthew 6:22: "The light of the body is the eye: if therefore thine eye be single, thy whole body shall be full of light." Friends have aspired to emulate this singleness of eye and focused purpose as part of the simplified life, and, at the same time, it leads them to avoid the duplicity which they believe would be acting "out of the truth."

Today, our Testimony of Simplicity may mean avoiding excesses in eating habits for reasons of health, and it may mean simplifying the use of our time by focusing on those things that are most important rather than being consumed by a hectic and stressful schedule.

Equality

Equality has always been important for Friends, but historically, and especially for Conservative Friends, it was because "God is no respecter of persons." So often the primary emphasis today is on "equal rights," which are derived from our sense of a common humanity. Allegedly Friends have always recognized the equality of women and men, especially in ministry and the life and work of the meeting, but their practice has not always been equal to their claim. For Friends, equality was derived from their belief that we are all created in the image of God and therefore are accountable to one another as children of one God. Comparatively speaking, Friends throughout their history have had an impressive record of treating all persons with equal respect and dignity. As a result Quakers have always been pioneers for social justice and equal opportunity for all. But they have had divergent views of how this equality is derived and theologically defined.

Plainness And Self-denial

We miss much of the mood of Conservative Wilburite Quakerism if we do not mention the way of "plainness and self-denial" that Wilburites believed was practiced by the early Friends after whom they patterned their lives. They believed this aspect of early Quakerism was part of the way the Christian life should be lived. The end of this road of commitment and faithfulness leads to what seventeenth-century Friends called "Christian perfection." It was what every Friend in the tradition of Fox, Penn, and Barclay was called to fulfill, just as a century later those who were followers of John and Charles Wesley in the Methodist movement were called to practice Christian perfection in their own faith community.

William Penn's *No Cross, No Crown* was for early Friends, and for Conservative Wilburite Friends two centuries later, a clarion call to become disciples of the living Christ. Penn said that we are to become "followers of the perfect Jesus, that most heavenly man."[28] And to be a disciple of Christ one needed to follow the admonition of Jesus: "If any man would come after me, let him deny himself and take up his cross and follow me" (Matt. 6: 24). For Friends this meant not only certain faith commitments, but it also called for a life of plainness and self-denial, and the avoidance of vain and empty customs.

Christian Perfection

As stated before, Robert Barclay's *Apology* also offered a model for Conservative Friends. He espoused the doctrine of Christian perfection referred to above, but he went on to say further:

> This is not a perfection that has no room for daily growth. It is by no means a claim to be pure, holy, and perfect as God. It is a perfection that is proportional to a man's requirements....

> Perhaps there are those who can say with certainty that they have attained this state. Personally I have to be modest and merely say that it is attainable, because I confess ingenuously

that I have not yet attained it. But that is no reason to deny that there is such a state.[29]

In the nineteenth and twentieth centuries, the doctrine of Christian perfection among Friends has taken two divergent forms. Those in the liberal tradition have couched it in the language of idealism, either philosophical or mystical. Critics of this, however, have called it unjustified optimism because it does not take into account human sin, which continually frustrates the achievement of ideal goals. At the other extreme has been the evangelical position (sometimes referred to as the Holiness tradition), which takes human sin seriously but believes, as did the Wesleyan Methodists, that by a second work of God's grace human beings can become sanctified and made holy in the sight of God. Robert Barclay seems to suggest that this kind of perfection is possible by the grace and power of God but is rarely reached, as he admitted in regard to his own life.

The Queries, Advices, and the Disciplines

One of the important ways Friends historically, and Conservative Friends in the nineteenth and twentieth centuries especially, maintained orderly discipline in the Religious Society of Friends was to regularly answer the Queries and read the Advices inherited from past generations of Friends. Queries and Advices embodied the faith and practice of Friends who had gone before and became the basis for the Book of Discipline, which included the more important Advices and rules of government.

Conservative Friends Books of Discipline were derived from the Orthodox Yearly Meeting Disciplines of the nineteenth century. These in turn had evolved from less well-defined guidelines for faith and practice in the eighteenth century. The Elders and Overseers were the guardians of the Book of Discipline, which has a history of its own among Friends.

A summary of the Queries and Advices by Philadelphia Arch Street Yearly Meeting, 1909 is very similar to the Disciplines followed by the Conservative Yearly Meetings:

> The proper attendance of religious meetings; the maintaining of Christian love to one another and of a behavior consistent with it; a careful, religious education and training of children; the observance of the testimonies of the Society in regard to plainness of speech and apparel, to moderation in business and in manner of living, as well as strict honesty, temperance, and punctuality; the assistance of such members as are in necessitious circumstances; the bearing of a faithful testimony against oaths and against all military services or engagements; a testimony to the spirituality of the gospel, and also to a ministry that depends upon the renewed guidance of the Holy Spirit upon every occasion when it is exercised, and that is without pecuniary reward; and finally, the exercise of a Christian spirit as well as of true authority in the treatment of offenders.[30]

The purpose of the Queries and Advices was to lift up a standard for Friends. Friends were to examine themselves regularly in order to determine whether members of the Society measured up to their religious profession. It was customary to read and answer in writing all eight Queries once a year in all subordinate meetings, prior to a summary report made to the Yearly Meeting. The First, Second and Eighth Queries were answered every three months and the results reported to the Quarterly Meeting. This practice developed into a pattern whereby all subordinate meetings were accountable to the Yearly

Meeting. (For a listing of Queries and Advices for Ohio Yearly Meeting Conservative see Appendices A and B.)

For many years the practice among Conservative Friends was that only "select" or fully recognized and accredited members be allowed to conduct the business of the meeting. The separate business meeting for Minister and Elders, on the other hand, defined "select" as only recorded ministers and elders who could attend and conduct the business of their meetings.

As a boy I remember with some consternation sitting through long hours of listening to the Queries and Advices being read and answered in our monthly meeting. Then we had to go through the same procedure in muarterly meeting every three months, and again in yearly meeting when all eight Queries were answered. Although the idea of accountability to a higher body seemed reasonable, the answers given each year were so similar that they were predictable. One longed for more variety and creativity in the answers given, as well as serious consideration as to whether Friends really measured up to their faith commitments.

Friends did not use the terms "freedom" and "order" as two contending principles in the free association of people in community, but these principles apply to churches and Friends meetings just as they do to secular associations and communities. In theory, however, Friends believed that if they followed what George Fox called "Gospel Order," they would be fulfilling their Christian responsibility and, at the same time, be brought into a common sense of unity. For Friends to be reconciled to one another meant seeking the Light of Christ together until they could corporately discern the mind of Christ, and thereby the will of God.

Puritan Influence on Friends' Outward Behavior

As evidenced by their adherence to testimonies and painstaking review of Queries and Advices, early Friends lived out their Christian faith in a scrupulous manner. No doubt puritanical influence upon these Friends helped shape their daily lives. It is not surprising, therefore, that Conservative Friends adopted many of these same customs and practiced them more or less consistently into the twentieth century.

In the seventeenth century, Barclay recommended a pattern and style of life for persons who were "leavened with the love of God" and had a "sense of his presence" in their lives. One important element of early Friends lifestyle was how one used the time God grants to each person. How did early Friends weave what we call "free time" into a life of purpose for the glory of God? The following is one of Barclay's examples:

> There are plenty of...forms of innocent recreation available which relax the mind sufficiently. Friends may visit one another. There is the reading of history, or serious conversation about present or past transactions. One can follow gardening, or use geometrical or mathematical experiments or other things of that nature.[31]

What is surprising is how *much* of this puritanical thought and behavior prevailed among Orthodox and Conservative Friends. This is evident from the following statements from *Principles of Quakerism*. Keep in mind that many Conservative Wilburite Friends maintained very similar puritanical practices well into the first half of the twentieth century, and some maintained them even longer.

Friends now believe that physical, mental and spiritual health are best promoted by a wide range of activities and interests, rather than by the continual introspection of the ascetics. Games belong especially to childhood, but there is no set period when childhood ends;...[But] if too much importance is attached to winning, especially in the case of interclass and interschool games, the feeling which is stirred up is often very unwholesome. Friends are opposed to all professional sports of all kinds. They believe that it is unworthy of a rational being to make sport the business of his life, and they therefore object to attendance at such games.…It is safe to say that professional sports have a strong tendency to demoralize those who participate in them, and to a less degree to demoralize the spectators.…

Secondly, Friends are opposed to theatre-going because of its effect on those who go. Everybody condemns bad plays, but who shall say where the line shall be drawn?

Another popular form of recreation which Friends condemn is dancing. Dancing belongs to a kind of social life which is at variance with Quaker ideals.…The psychological facts involved need not be discussed here, but those who have studied the subject most carefully...are of the opinion that the tendency of mixed dances is distinctly harmful.

Playing-cards are so generally used for gambling that they are fairly esteemed as gamblers' tools, and therefore likely to lead to evil associations.… Friends do not generally object to...games [which] call for skill of hand, and such games often have real value as training.…[But] games of pure chance are very objectionable, because of their tendency to foster the gambling spirit.

The outdoor recreation of adults, such as travel, camping, and the various kinds of nature study, afford valuable physical and intellectual stimulus and recreation in the best sense, and

Friends generally believe that a small part of one's time may properly be spent in such things if he can afford it. The study of botany and other natural sciences afford delightful recreation, and, at the same time if pursued in a reverent spirit, promotes spiritual growth.

To sum up: Friends recognize the value of recreation. They believe that one should choose such recreations…as are within his means and will best promote his health of body, mind and soul.[32]

The puritanical and Spartan lifestyle counseled by Orthodox and Conservative Friends of nearly a century ago will seem extreme, maybe even unacceptable, to Friends today, including a majority of Conservative Friends. But perhaps the lesson for us is to consider our priorities more carefully in the stewardship of God's time.

Passing on the Faith from One Generation to the Next

Friends from the early period had schools under the care of the meeting for their children. It was not until the second half of the twentieth century that they began having First Day schools in their meetings. Many Conservative Friends had some form of family worship and/or Bible reading each day. On First Day afternoons it was customary for some families to have a quiet time in the home devoted to reading together the early writings of Friends, particularly from the journals of Friends ministers, or from the Philadelphia *Friend*.

Of course, the primary way of learning was by observing the examples of parents, older siblings, grandparents, and close relatives who often lived with the family. As Kathryn Damiano suggests, this method of learning was "catching Quakerism by osmosis," a gradual, often unconscious process of assimilation. As noted earlier, most of the Friends primary schools were laid down during the 1920s and 30s. But since then a new concern and interest has arisen among Quakers in general to start up Friends schools again, as well as to do some home schooling. This is increasingly so because parents are not satisfied with the public schools and their influence on their children. Thus, even though Conservative Friends have made significant changes in the past two or three generations, they still hold onto many aspects of a "guarded education" for their children.

1. *A Brief Syinopsis of the Principles of the Religious Society of Friends* (hereafter referred to as *Brief Synopsis*), with minutes of adoption from the Yearly Meetings (Conservative) of New England, Canada, Ohio, Western (Indiana), Iowa, Kansas and North Carolina. (Barnesville, Ohio: adopted 1912, published 1913), p.8.

2. *Ibid.*, pp.8-9

3. John Wilbur, *Letters to George Crosfield* (Providence:J.A. and R.A. Reid, Printers, 1879), p.30.

4. *Ibid.*, pp. 31-32.

5. *Ibid.*, p. 49.

6. *Principles of Quakerism*, Issued by the Representatives of the Religious Society of Friends of Pennsylvania, New Jersey and Delaware. (Philadelphia: Friends Book Store, 1909), p. 26.

7. *Brief Synopsis*, p. 12.

8. *Ibid.*, pp. 25-26.

9. Robert Barclay, *Barclay's Apology in Modern English*. Edited by Dean Freiday (Elberron, N.J.: Private printing, 1967), p. 50.

10. *Ibid.*, p. 58.

11. *Ibid.*, p. 60.

12. *Brief Synopsis*, p. 27.

13. *Ibid.*, p. 13.

14. *Ibid.*, p. 14.
15. *Principles of Quakerism*, p. 107.
16. *Barclay's Apology*, p. 254.
17. *Principles of Quakerism*, p. 114.
18. *Principles of Quakerism*, pp. 114-115.
19. *Brief Synopsis*, pp. 18-19.
20. *Principles of Quakerism*, pp. 121-123.
21. *Ibid.*, p. 122.
22. *Brief Synopsis*, p. 22.
23. T. Canby Jones, "George Fox and the Interpretation of the Sacraments," (Private printing), pp. 1,4,7.
24. Wilmer A. Cooper, *A Living Faith: An Historical Study of Quaker Beliefs*, (Richmond, Indiana: Friends United Press, 1990), p. 101.
25. *Brief Synopsis*, p. 24.
26. *Principles of Quakerism*, p. 138.
27. *Brief Synopsis*, pp. 27-28.
28. William Penn, *No Cross, No Crown* (Philadelphia: T.K. and P.G. Collins, 1853), p. 85.
29. Dean Freiday, *Barclay's Apology*, pp. 156-57.
30. *Principles of Quakerism*, pp. 206-208.
31. *Barclay's Apology*, pp. 410-11.
32. *Principles of Quakerism*, pp. 195-99.

Chapter Three

Growing
Up
Plain

As a young boy growing up in a Conservative Friends home and community, I had a clear feeling of the greatness and goodness of God.

As I look back on this, it is something of a surprise to me—especially since I chose to break away from that community and its expectations at a fairly young age. Nevertheless, this was the view of the created universe that I experienced.

We did go through some very hard times, especially during the Great Depression—1929 and most of the 1930s. But even though I knew of bad things that happened in the larger world, and sometimes in our community, it never occurred to me to ask, "Why do bad things happen to good people?"—the theme of Harold S. Kushner's small book (1981) on the problem of good and evil and how to reconcile that with a good and loving God.

As a boy, it just seemed to me that the world as looked at from the earth with the blue sky and the sun and moon and stars above constituted a friendly and supportive life here in this vast universe. For this I was, and continue to be, thankful, even though I have learned since that the natural world, as well as the world of people, can be much more unfriendly, violent and destructive than I was able to comprehend then.

During those years I thought of myself as basically a good boy, even though I sometimes gave way to temptation, which in our belief system we attributed to the work of Satan. One day, about age four, I found a gallon of red paint that I opened and then used to paint the black leather seats of our Model T Ford car. Fortunately, I was caught before I had gotten very far, so that much of the damage could be undone. I must have been disciplined at the time, but I don't seem to remember about that.

When I was three or four years older, I was standing in front of our house one day when a car came along the road with a man passing out leaflets. These were undoubtedly advertisements of some sort. At the edge of our village, the car turned around and came back, and as it came by I tore up the flyer we received so that the driver could observe what I was doing. Fortunately, he did not stop and reprimand me, but he had hardly disappeared when I had severe pangs of conscience for my actions.

As I have reflected on the incident in later years, I believe it had partly to do with our Conservative Friends presumption that everything outside our comfortable little community was suspect and antithetical to our particular set of beliefs and practices. In other words, I must have thought that this strange man from outside our community didn't belong there, and that anything he was distributing must be part of the tainted world outside.

But how did I reconcile all this with my earlier reference to the goodness of the world and of God's loving care? Well,

I'm not sure, except that I held my experience of God and the beauty of nature in one compartment of my mind, while in another part I became aware of a peopled world of various cultures and traditions that conflicted with God's world. That realization represented to me one of the paradoxes of life, which in my mature years I have come to believe is the way much of life is. Paradox, this reality of life, boggles the rational mind, which always demands consistency and order.

My extended family's entrance into the Ohio Conservative Friends community began at the turn of the twentieth century, when my Cooper family forebears moved from Chester County, Pennsylvania (southwest of Philadelphia) to Columbiana County, in east-central Ohio. My father, Walter M. Cooper (1870-1950), was the youngest of ten children. He and two older brothers and four sisters made this trek from the Orthodox Philadelphia Yearly Meeting (Arch Street) to Ohio Yearly Meeting (Conservative).

My father's eldest brother, Cyrus Cooper, who for all practical purposes was the patriarch of the family, made the first foray to Ohio Yearly Meeting at Barnesville, Ohio, in 1897. Because the family was increasingly uneasy about some of the progressivism of Philadelphia Orthodox Friends, they were in search of a place among Friends where they could feel that the "ancient testimonies" of Friends were honored and practiced. In Ohio Yearly Meeting (Conservative) they believed they had found such a place.

When they arrived in Ohio, these members of our extended family first settled in the neighborhood of Salem, Ohio, which was central to the northern quarterly meeting of Ohio Yearly Meeting (Conservative). Salem is approximately ninety miles upstate from Barnesville, the yearly meeting's unofficial headquarters. Barnesville is also the location of Olney Friends School (formerly known as Friends Boarding School), which has been until recently under the care of Ohio Conservative Friends. Some of the Cooper brothers and sisters brought their spouses with them from Pennsylvania, while others, including my father, found their "life mates" among Conservative Friends in Ohio.

My father met my mother, Anna P. Blackburn, when he came from Pennsylvania for the wedding of my Uncle Harry Cooper and Ruth Satterthwaite from Winona, Ohio. My mother was then a teacher at the Conservative Friends Primary School at Salem, Ohio. She had been raised on a farm fourteen miles southeast, near the unincorporated village of Middleton, Ohio, which formerly was known by the post office name of Mosk, Ohio.

Mother came from a family of six children, four girls and two boys. After attending Friends schools in Ohio she went to Westtown Boarding School near Philadelphia for additional training. This helped to prepare her for teaching at Friends Primary School at Salem.

Following my parents' marriage, Third Month 23, 1905, they served on the staff of the Tunesasseh Indian School in western New York state, which was founded and supported by Friends from Philadelphia. Father worked in the dairy while mother taught the Indian children.

We have only one picture of my parents at the Tunesasseh Indian School. They weren't there too long. I wish I could talk with them now about a lot of things—how they learned about the school, for instance. The school was a kind of mission. Philadelphia Yearly Meeting was originally responsible for starting the work in that particular part of the state and for starting that school. My parents must have learned of it from Philadelphia Yearly Meeting, since my father came from that area and my mother did go to Westtown School in the East. I know that it was the first thing they did in their married life, but I don't know if it was just another job or if they felt a particular call to it.

After a brief stay at the school my parents moved back to Middleton, where they were joined by Uncle Cyrus and Aunt Bertha and their son Samuel, who moved from Salem to Middleton to take up residence and work. This move apparently took place in 1907. There was a well-established Conservative Friends meeting at Middleton to which they felt drawn.

Uncle Cyrus started a general store in his home, which he operated for nearly ten years. At that point, in 1917, Uncle Cyrus returned to the carpentry trade, which he had practiced back east. After a half dozen years he again entered the store business forming a partnership with another Conservative Friend, David Morlan. They opened what became the Rural Supply Store at Middleton to serve rural families for several miles round. They sold everything from hardware, to feed, to groceries, to drygoods and much more. After it had become a thriving business, the groceries and drygoods were separated into another store across the street, run initially by Kenneth Morse, a plain Conservative Friend who had moved from Cleveland, Ohio to join Middleton Friends. The grocery and drygoods store, however, was later taken back by Cyrus Cooper. At this point the Rural Supply partnership was sold to Cyrus' son, Samuel Cooper, in partnership with my older brother, James R. Cooper.

When my father and mother settled at Middleton, they lived next door to the Friends meetinghouse, and two doors away from Uncle Cyrus and Aunt Bertha. In view of the close proximity of the residences, it seemed that my father was frequently under the scrutiny of his respected elder brother, a recorded Friends minister, as long as he lived.

Partly because we lived next door to the Middleton Friends Meetinghouse, my father was asked to be its caretaker.

He cleaned the building as needed for First Day and Fifth Day meetings for worship. In the winter he built fires in two pot-bellied stoves—one each on the men's and women's sides of the meetinghouse. Not far from the meetinghouse stood the one-room Friends Primary School for all eight grades, which our Friends children attended.

For a livelihood, my father started making brooms, which was a trade he had learned from his father. Gradually he coupled this with market gardening, and he discontinued broom making. Eventually he added a greenhouse and mushroom growing to the business. He did not feel comfortable, however, about raising flowers, especially cut flowers, so he concentrated on vegetable plants and hothouse tomatoes.

Uncle Harry, on the other hand, along with his son Charles at Salem, not only went into the greenhouse flower business but also into the cut-flower business in a major way. There was always some concern within the Cooper family whether a Conservative Friend could in good conscience be in the cut-flower business. There was a sense that it was not right to cut life off from its roots. And some felt it was not consistent with the historic Friends testimony of "plainness and self-denial." Even growing hothouse tomatoes in the greenhouse seemed like a luxury, because not everyone could afford to buy them. We marketed the tomatoes mostly in Youngstown, Ohio, twenty miles to the north where more affluent people lived who could afford them in off-season months of the year.

I am the youngest of my parents' five children and the only one to make a permanent break from the Conservative Friends community. I was born at home in 1920, as we all had been. I was apparently named for a "Wilmer" in my father's family who died young, but the truth is that I never liked the name and wished I could change it. In later years I chose a shortened version, "Wil," not to be confused with "Will" for

William and other like-sounding derivatives—including Wilma, which I dislike the most. I often receive mail addressed to "Wilma" Cooper!

My sister Sara (1907-1996) did not marry until her later years. On Fifth Month 18, 1991 at age 83, she married a former Friends Boarding School acquaintance, Howard Stratton from Flushing, Ohio, a widower. Brother James (1909-1990) married his Boarding School classmate, Bertha L. Hall from Winona, Ohio, on Eighth Month 23, 1935. In 1990 James died after a five-year battle with cancer. Brother Thomas (1911-1997) was married to Mildred Stanley Third Month 23, 1938 from the Gurney Friends Ohio Yearly Meeting at Damascus, Ohio. Another brother, Barclay (b.1915), died of whooping cough in infancy.

Middleton was a sparsely settled rural village of perhaps a hundred people. It was located on State Route 7, halfway between the industrial steel city of Youngstown to the north and East Liverpool located on the Ohio River to the south. We were about eight miles west of the Ohio-Pennsylvania line. Our mail came by rural delivery from Columbiana, Ohio, four miles northwest. The only other businesses in the village, besides the Cooper general store, our greenhouse and roadside market, and a blacksmith shop, was a gasoline station and auto repair garage run by Howard Cope, a member of our meeting who never attended.

One way to understand the Quaker nature of this community is to compare it with an Old Mennonite or Amish community. Indeed, we were located only a few miles from a Mennonite settlement where "plain people" lived and horse drawn buggies were to be seen on the roadways. Middleton was somewhat in transition when I was growing up, because buggies were being replaced by Model T Fords, or other makes of cars. Mud roads were beginning to be graveled and a few were paved. I can remember when State Road 7 was built through Middleton. It became a busy two-lane concrete highway between Lake Erie to the north and the Ohio River. Trucks hauling coal went north to the steel mills while steel was hauled south to the Ohio River for shipment.

Our Friends community was basically a separate culture unto itself. About the only place it connected with the world around was through our business contacts, which were essential for the survival of both. Just as the quietistic Friends of the eighteenth century tried to separate themselves from "the world" like the Mennonites and Amish did, so most Conservative Friends settlements in eastern Ohio "hedged" themselves in from the people around them. I sensed that "the world out there" could easily encroach on the purity of our religious faith and practice if we mingled too much with these folk.

For the most part we practiced Quaker plainness in dress and address, which meant that we used the traditional "thee" and "thou" personal pronouns when we addressed one another and the public. Of course the original testimony was to avoid social distinction in Old England, but almost no one understood that in my community. When I accompanied my father on business trips, I would become embarrassed when he insisted on using the "plain language" to persons who often did not understand what he was trying to say. He tried to maintain consistency in his use of the "plain language" out of a sense of duty.

Our house was not large. It didn't seem crowded for a family our size in those days, but it would seem crowded now. It was a two-story house with four bedrooms and outside toilet facilities. When I was young, we still had kerosene lamps. The fireplace we had when I was a child is still in the house as it stands today, currently under restoration by my nephew.

My mother shaped our home a good deal in terms of a

pretty simple life, clothing and that kind of thing. We didn't have anything fancy around the windows; plain windows with a shade were part of the testimony of simplicity.

The life that my parents and the Conservative Friends community believed in living was pretty hum-drum. The message I got was: life's a serious business and you'd better be living every moment for the Lord. My mother really depended on her leading of the Spirit, even moment by moment. You were a little suspect if you laughed too much; life was a very sober kind of business.

Both at home and in school I was never exposed to the fairy tales and children's stories with which most youth grow up. I was not allowed to take part in school plays, and theater-going was forbidden. I remember the first movie I went to see with some school friends during vacation from Friends Boarding School (unbeknown to my family, of course). I felt so guilty that I was sure the theater was going to collapse or burn down before I got out!

As Conservative Friends my family did not observe any of the usual holidays, including those of both church and state. This meant no Advent and Christmas celebration, and no Lenten or Easter observances. At our Friends one-room school I remember when I first learned from another Quaker school friend (whose family was less strict than mine) that there was a Santa Claus! Just before Christmas one year, he told me that if I would hang up my stockings at the fireplace Santa would come down the chimney and fill them on Christmas Eve.

I went home with great excitement and proceeded to hang up my stockings as my friend instructed me. My parents noted what I was doing, so there was some question about how to handle the situation. They let me finish my preparation, apparently believing I would learn my lesson.

I spent a sleepless night imagining that I heard Santa

coming down the chimney. The result, of course, was that my parents were right after all. My Quaker school friends had deceived me, because if there really were a Santa, he would have filled my stockings! My Father *did* place some chunks of coal in the socks, whether to punish me or humor me, I do not know. At any rate I had to explain to my school friends that Santa Claus was a figment of the imagination.

Also in the tradition of early Friends, my parents refused to allow any music in our home. Music was forbidden in the meetinghouse and schoolhouse as well. But my older brother Thomas somehow acquired a harmonica and brought it home. As soon as my father discovered it, he proceeded to throw it into the open fireplace in front of us children—a very painful experience I shall never forget!

Because our community was made up of mainly Conservative Friends, it was they and their children with whom we had most of our interaction. On some First Day afternoons, we would drive to nearby communities to visit relatives.

My closest playmate as a child was my first cousin, Alfred Carter, my mother's nephew who lived nearby. For some reason we were materialistically minded in our play. We made play money and, in our imagination, bought and sold cars.

One of the few special events and sources of joy I had to look forward to was quarterly meeting, held every three months, at the Salem Friends Meetinghouse. The Conservative Friends community would not have admitted the social nature of these meetings, but that was certainly an element of them. I remember the food.

After meeting for worship and a long tedious business meeting (especially once a year when we read and answered all eight Queries in the Conservative Friends Discipline), we had a quarterly meeting lunch. The food was prepared on trays, stacked on portable wooden racks, and carried from the deserted Friends schoolhouse next door to the meeting room where we ate together and visited. What a treat: ham sandwiches on soft buns, freshly made apple sauce and cookies, served with tea, coffee or hot water (with milk) for the grown folks.

I also looked forward to going with my father or brothers to market our produce. This gave me a view of "the world out there," which otherwise I knew very little about. I was able to see how city folks lived as compared with us country folks. We sold produce among many different European ethnic groups, Negroes (as we called them then), and Jewish people. I'm afraid I developed some prejudices against the Jewish merchants because they usually outbid my father in business dealings.

There are less pleasant memories during the Great Depression. To make a living we sometimes bought apples from nearby orchards and peddled them in the steel mill towns in and around Youngstown to the north, along the Ohio River to the south, and up the river toward Pittsburgh. We also built a special trailer on our pickup truck to haul coal from the mines nearby to sell to poor people in the steel mill towns.

I shall never forget the depressing images of the countless people and their children who lived in poverty, often without work. We, too, were sometimes deprived and on the edge of despair during the Depression years when my father hardly knew how to provide food for our family. Once we knew of a man nearby who had nothing but potato peelings to carry to work in his lunch pail. So my boyhood days are filled with both good and bad memories. But we survived, and today we sometimes wonder how our children and grandchildren will make it even in comparatively good times.

Our meeting, like most Conservative Friends meetings in those days, did not believe in First Day Schools for the purpose of teaching the Bible and giving moral and religious instruction. Rather, we had daily Bible reading in our home, everyday after breakfast, with a time for quiet reflection and prayer. Also, at our Locust Knoll Friends School we had to memorize verses from the Bible and recite them before going to meeting at 10:30 every Fifth Day morning. This constituted our religious instruction in our community, in place of the Sunday Schools of other churches. Added to this was my mother's teaching about proper behavior and spiritual practice, passed along in part by her method of childhood discipline.

When I was eight or nine years old, I clearly initiated a deceptive act that soon caught up with me. Howard Cope's gas station and auto repair shop was located within easy walking distance of our home. Because Howard Cope, a disaffected member of our meeting, also sold chewing tobacco, cigars and cigarettes, and because one could expect to hear swearing and bad language used at the garage, it was a place my parents did not want me to go. There were times, however, when I had to run errands there. I had clear instructions not to hang around.

My misdeed was to make unannounced trips to Cope's Garage. When no one was looking I would quietly sneak in and grab a handful of match packets from the counter, which of course were free for those who smoked. At the time I tried to justify my actions by reminding myself that I was taught that the use of tobacco in any form was a sin, so maybe I was helping to restrain this evil practice! I continued to run off with the matches until one day my mother discovered a large pile of them under my bed in my upstairs room. I had been caught red-handed and was forced to give my mother a full explanation.

My mother was wise in how she dealt with me. She collected the matches and said I should go with her to Howard Cope and apologize to him for what I had done. That was a very hard thing for me to do, but I did go with her and, after my apology, I felt shamed but forgiven and reconciled. Nevertheless, the experience taught me a lesson that has served me well ever since.

Another lesson my mother taught me had to do with a craze I had for ice cream. Howard Cope's gas station was the only place in Middleton to buy ice cream—a well known Isalys brand made in Youngstown, Ohio. What a treat—one dip for five cents and two dips for ten cents! I did little chores around the house and yard to earn my pennies and nickels. (One task I remember vividly was to pull deep-rooted plantain out of the yard for a penny each.)

But even when I had the money to buy the ice cream, my mother tried to discipline my endless craving by teaching me another lesson. Before I could go after an ice cream cone, she asked me to go to my room to pray about it to see whether I could discern God's will in the matter. The irony of this was that God and I usually worked it out so that I could get my ice cream! Although my mother probably questioned my "deal" with God, she allowed me to act on the outcome of my prayer in order to teach me that it was important to take things to God in prayer and then live with the consequences, for good or ill.

I was a fairly independent child. I think my parents always thought of me as difficult, not willing to give my will up to the will of the Lord. They didn't have any understanding of child development as we theorize about it today. (Although, I don't know that we're any more successful!)

At any rate, I was always made to sit with my father on the facing bench in meeting, perhaps to assure proper behavior. My parents never spoke in meeting for worship, but my father would speak in meeting for business.

Uncle Cyrus, who sat on the bench above and behind my father and me in meeting, *did* speak often in meeting. He ministered in the traditional Conservative sing-song style, and I well remember him quaking with the power of the Spirit as he spoke. We children sometimes tried to reproduce those experiences as we "played" meeting for worship later for our own entertainment.

Just as powerful for me were mid-week meetings on Fifth Day when usually nothing was spoken. People would close businesses at mid-morning and children would come from school for those meetings. You could sometimes really tell the moving of the Spirit. There was a genuine sense of the moving of the presence of Christ in our midst, which left us with a feeling of spiritual unity—what Friends have called "a covered meeting." I learned that from very early on.

My other vivid childhood memory of that meetinghouse stems from an incident when I was perhaps seven or eight years old. I became very unhappy with my family and decided to run away from home. My plan was to get up early in the morning, climb out my upstairs window, and slowly and quietly scoot down the cable which was the telephone connection to our old-fashioned wall phone.

Having accomplished that safely, I then had to decide where I was going. Apparently I hadn't given that much thought, so on the spur of the moment I decided to run up to the meetinghouse and hide underneath a bench in the gallery. I waited it out there until I could decide my next move. Daylight soon arrived, and I had to continue lying in my uncomfortable position for what seemed like a very long time.

When my parents and siblings missed me at breakfast, they decided to start hunting. After two or three hours of looking, they checked the meetinghouse. There the search ended when they found me underneath the bench. The prodigal son had to return home much humiliated—I had not really pulled this thing off! My parents saw the whole episode as childish behavior and let my humiliation be the only consequence.

I, like my father, often felt the watchful eye of my Uncle Cyrus. I can remember that on my first day of school when I was six years old, I had to stop by my Uncle Cyrus' store, probably to buy a tablet and pencil. As I was leaving, Uncle Cyrus said, "Wilmer, thee must be a good example to the other children."

I believe there was even a little suspicion that our Cooper family, who represented the most conservative element in the Friends community, might be unduly influenced by others in the school who had more interaction with "the world" than we did. After all, Uncle Cyrus' only child was partially taught at home by his mother for fear he might be wrongly influenced by the other children, even in our Friends school. I learned in later years that much of this was motivated by the quietistic Friends principle of a "guarded education."

At the end of my fourth grade, when I was ten years old, an important change came in our Friends community. Our primary school had dwindled to ten students, all boys. Glenn Rockwell, a Conservative Friend from Fairhope, Alabama, who had been our teacher for my first four years, left the community. His leaving—combined with the small enrollment—meant the school had to be laid down. This situation produced a crisis in our family.

Parents of the other nine boys planned for their children to go by bus to the Fairfield Centralized School three miles away. The father of three of the boys was on the public school board and was encouraging this move. The day school opened my parents, especially my father, could not bear to let me go on the school bus to the public school. In fact, they kept me out for a couple of days to pray over the matter and seek some clear guidance from the Lord about what to do.

Finally, contrary to my father's wishes, it was decided that my brother Thomas would drive me in the old Ford to the public school and let me out, with a note of explanation to the teacher and school principal. I would be wearing the "plain dress" as my family did, of course, which always set us apart from the surrounding community.

As we arrived at Fairfield Centralized School, which had a student body of several hundred, the school buses were arriving with what seemed to me like throngs of children who poured into the school building.

Although it was a place I had never set foot in before, my brother just told me to get out and try to find the fifth grade room. I realized I had to be brave and, for the first time, thrust my way into "the world out there" that I knew so little about and had been admonished to view with some caution. I had to ask two or three times before I found my classroom on the second floor. I approached the teacher with my note from my parents; she treated me kindly, and showed me to an empty seat. There were probably forty students in my room, which seemed very threatening to me.

I don't remember much more about that day except that when I returned home that afternoon my family was still unclear whether I should return the next day. I did return, however, and that day I learned to ride the school bus with children from the larger community, some of whom seemed rowdy in behavior.

To add to my parents' dilemmas, a decision had to be made about my participation in a required music class at school. Again I had to take a note from my parents to the teacher and the principal asking that I be excused from the class. That request placed them in an awkward position because of having to decide what I was to do while the class was meeting and singing daily. At this point my parents compromised and agreed to let me sit in the class but not have a music book along with the other children. Certainly I was not to join in singing with the others. Somehow I endured and survived all that, but it is no wonder I can't read a single musical note today! Fortunately my teacher tried to treat me with understanding and care.

One of the trials I couldn't quite endure was being made fun of on the school bus or on the playground because of my plain Quaker attire. I dreaded facing this each day. Sometimes I was called "Cyrus" by the other boys, because the community knew my uncle was a strict, plain-dressed Friends minister and storekeeper at Middleton. This deeply offended and hurt me.

When the cold weather set in, my parents allowed me to substitute a knit wool cap for my plain hat. The cap could be turned down over my ears and buttoned around my neck, which was acceptable because other children had similar knit caps for the cold weather. But what was I to do when the warm spring days came? I wasn't allowed to go without anything on my head, as many others were. I decided to sweat it out with that hot wool cap until school was out in the spring. I was determined not to wear my plain hat to school again if there were any way of avoiding it.

This forced change of schools, which also forced me to mix with "the world's people," proved to be an almost unbearable culture shock for me. I am convinced that the experience triggered my hand tremor, a trait which I probably inherited from my mother's side of the family.

Since—as I've already mentioned—I did not arrive on the first day of school that year as the rest of the children did, the teacher gave me a seat in the back of the room, in the very last row. The principal of the school used to visit classes just to observe. He was a pretty stern sort of man, and for some reason he very often used to come by and stand behind my desk.

Of course, I knew what he was doing, but I got the strange feeling that maybe he was watching me! We were writing, and I started having trouble with the tremor immediately.

About the same time, I went to the bank to withdraw five dollars out of a savings account. I had to sign for it, and I could hardly do it. I have had many situations over the years when I couldn't sign my name. On one of my trips to Africa, I wasn't sure how I'd get signed out of my hotel, but the clerk finally signed me out. I have recently found a medication that takes care of this tremor, but I spent years doing all kinds of things to avoid situations that would make it noticeable.

Because that fifth grade year was so difficult for me, my family looked for other possibilities. A partial solution presented itself when my older brother James was invited to become the teacher at the Conservative Friends Primary School at Damascus, Ohio, five miles west of Salem and about twenty miles from our home. I went with him, and we stayed during the week with my Aunt Lydia Woolman, one of my father's sisters who had migrated to Ohio with the family at the turn of the century and who lived on a farm about three miles out of town. The school stood next to the Upper Springfield Meetinghouse at Damascus, next to the Conservative Friends burial ground. Unlike the school in Middleton, there was a mixture of girls and boys in this school, though it was also small.

This school away from home became part of my educational experience for the next two years, the sixth and seventh grades. The second year my brother and I drove back and forth from Middleton on a daily basis rather than boarding with Aunt Lydia. By the end of that period, the Damascus Friends decided they could not support their small school any longer, and like the Friends at Middleton, they laid the school down.

The only recourse was to return to the Fairfield Centralized School that I had attended before. My eighth-grade year there was not the rending experience of my fifth-grade year. I had the previous experience to build on, and I was a little older and better able to deal with the difficulties I encountered. In fact, during that year I took on a kind of boldness uncharacteristic of my family and me.

For some reason, I do not recall the details now, the students that year were in rebellion against the school superintendent for certain administrative decisions and regulations in the school. One bright spring day, the majority of the students went on strike by walking out and spending most of the day on the playground. Persuaded by the majority, I joined in. This, however, got me into trouble at home.

One of the school board members was a respected and weighty Friend in our meeting, and because his children were in the school and did not go out on strike, word got back to my parents that I had. Although I was disciplined, the incident eventually blew over and the superintendent was maintained in his job. I do not believe, however, that I ever regained the full acceptance and respect of the school board member of our meeting.

My father was very committed to the Conservative agenda to keep alive the "ancient testimonies and practices" of Friends as expressed in Robert Barclay's *Apology* and William Penn's *No Cross, No Crown*, as well as the Bible. But he—like me as I grew older—apparently was not always happy with the constraints this commitment placed upon him. He always felt duty-bound to keep the faith and not waiver because of Uncle Cyrus' weight as a respected, recorded minister in Ohio Yearly Meeting.

Like many other Conservative Friends, however, Father experienced an inner uncertainty about the quietistic mood and stance of Wilburite Friends. Sometimes meeting for worship was so quiet that it was dull and lifeless and lacked religious fervor and spiritual satisfaction. Although Father, as an elder, was constantly under the scrutiny of Uncle Cyrus to maintain the proper standards of an elder in the meeting, he at times hungered for something more than he was getting at Middleton Friends Meeting.

Although I am not sure how my father learned about some of the camp meetings of holiness religious groups held in our part of Ohio, he had a secret desire to attend some of them and hear their preaching and hymn singing. Unbeknown to Uncle Cyrus, who lived two doors away, on a few occasions father suggested that on First Day afternoon we drive to one of these camp meetings, usually some miles away.

My brother Thomas, later a recorded minister in Ohio Yearly Meeting, also had a yearning for this kind of religious experience, as well as did my sister Sara. Both of them were somewhat under the influence of my Aunt Elma Carter, my mother's sister who had left our meeting over an unhappy incident in the community. As a result, she had joined a Nazarene church some miles from Middleton. For several years my sister Sara followed in the footsteps of Aunt Elma, and for a short time she attended Cleveland Bible College under the care of Gurneyite Friends of the Holiness persuasion.

When the opportunity came to join in one of these journeys to a Holiness camp meeting, I usually went along for the ride. I do not remember whether my mother came along or not, and my older brother James was more reserved and less inclined toward such adventures. In any event, one summer First Day afternoon, several of us departed in our Model T Ford touring car to attend a camp meeting in Sebring, Ohio, some twenty-five miles away.

As we were going through Washingtonville on the way, a man in another Model T Ford barged out of a side alley onto the road and nearly collided with us. We suspected he was probably drunk. I could immediately see that my father wondered whether this was a sign from the Lord that we should not go on. But about a mile up the road we had a flat tire, and sure enough that was a *clear* sign we were not meant to attend the camp meeting. After repairing the tire we turned around and went home, feeling somewhat cheated by our First Day afternoon excursion.

A similar but different incident sticks in my mind to this day as indicative of my father's yearning to be faithful to Friends tradition even while he felt the need for a little religious excitement, which Conservative Friends did not provide. Probably I was a couple of years older then and was beginning to drive the Model T Ford. (In those days there were no driver's licenses required and no minimum age limit.)

On another First Day afternoon, father had seen a notice of a Holiness camp meeting at Wellsville, Ohio, down the Ohio River about twenty-five miles from us. He asked if I would like to drive him to the camp meeting in our recently acquired 1925 black Ford coupe. To the best of my knowledge no one, except Mother perhaps, knew that we took off. I don't believe Father wanted Uncle Cyrus or other ministers and elders of the meeting to know. After a long drive we arrived at the camp grounds. The meeting was already underway, and the grounds were nearly full of people and vehicles. Father suggested that we drive as close to the large tent meeting as possible, but he felt more comfortable sitting in the car and not going into the meeting.

By opening the windows we were able to hear the singing, the preaching, and the altar call. But before it was all over father felt we should leave and not make ourselves conspicuous. So off we drove home. No flat tires or near mishaps this time! I believe my father manifested something of a guilty conscience for having done this, but also a satisfaction that he had heard some strong preaching and singing, which made the heart glad.

These incidents were not unlike what takes place even today among some Conservative Friends. From time to time members of the meeting feel a dryness and lifelessness in their times of worship, although they would be very reluctant to give up the silent waiting upon the Lord and the visitation of the Holy Spirit in ministry and prayer. In recent years, whole families have come and gone from Conservative Friends because of their hankering for something more. Since the 1960s, with the great wave of heightened spirituality emanating from the Pentecostal and charismatic movements, some Conservative Friends have been influenced by other styles of Christian faith and practice.

This influence has often been very confusing, particularly to the young people who have been puzzled about what to believe and whom to follow. Their experiences have sometimes involved faith healing meetings and perhaps occasional speaking in tongues (glossolalia). Although these manifestations have not been entirely alien to Friends historically, they have been frowned upon by most Friends who are more traditionally conservative. Sometimes this has been a source of friction and division in meetings, and has been cause for confusion because members have not always understood the faith and practice of authentic Quakerism. Some loss of membership has come as a result.

My family's sometime-interest in Holiness-style worship when I was a boy parallels that of some Conservative Friends today who are drawn to Holiness and evangelical churches. Both of these forays into more emotional styles of worship reflect something similar to the unrest among Orthodox Friends in the nineteenth century who turned from the quiet ways of historic Quakerism to more evangelical and Holiness patterns of pastoral/programmed worship and ministry. This is not to say that a move toward more Holiness-style worship is the future direction of Conservative Friends, but we need to be aware that, because of the continued decline in their numbers, Conservative Friends often look elsewhere for more productive examples of Christian faithfulness.

When I went away to Friends Boarding School at Barnesville, Ohio, for my high school education, there was still a substantial amount of plainness exhibited in the lifestyle and governance of the school. It was at this point that I began to change my "plain dress" by wearing a tie; however, I was not allowed to have buttons on my sleeves or cuffs on my trousers. But more important, at Friends Boarding School I was exposed to the traditional "guarded education" of Friends in ways that continued to mold my life. Again, this reflected the Conservative Friends ethos which I believe is rooted in eighteenth-century Quaker Quietism.

We were not allowed to read any fiction in our English literature classes. Already I have indicated how I was denied exposure to good music and music appreciation, which continued at FBS during my student days. All my life I have deeply regretted being deprived of a first-hand acquaintance with the arts in my educational experiences. This deficiency clearly showed up in my low scores in the arts, drama, and literature parts of the Graduate Record Exams for entrance to university graduate studies.

Although my family's Conservative Friends background never allowed for too much fun in life, I did manage to have a bit of it at boarding school. I was not very good at sports, but in the fall of the year I played soccer, usually in the halfback or fullback position, and in the spring I played baseball and tried to become a catcher. In the winter and spring I joined the hiking contest and earned my "Olney" letter completing three hundred miles in six weeks. I also ran the hundred yard dash.

Following noon and evening meals in the dining room, I often joined those who raced as fast as we could to get a place at one of the carom tables in the boys' dorm. Radios were scarce and not generally allowed. But Seventh Day evening we were allowed to crowd into Teacher Byron Thomas' office to listen to the school's one radio. To the consternation of Teacher Byron, we usually listened to cowboy music from Wheeling, West Virginia.

After meals we were allowed to walk up to the Stillwater Yearly Meetinghouse and back again on the brick walk, and on First Day after meeting it was customary for nearly everyone to walk two by two before dinner to the Taber Farm and back, nearly a mile away. Girls and boys were allowed to have supervised gym exhibitions and relay games on Seventh Day evenings in the old barn-like gym. At the end of the evening we were allowed to pair up with girls (if we were "lucky") to walk them between the gym and the Collecting Room in the main building. There we always had Evening Collection with the Superintendent reading a chapter from the Bible.

On First Day afternoons we had to be in our rooms for Quiet Hour from two to three o'clock, before going for walks or other approved activities. Brothers and sisters and cousins were allowed to sit together and visit in the Collecting Room once a week after supper. My cousin Elinor Jones (Mother's niece from Iowa) and I met on those occasions. A "forbidden" activity that I was drawn into was playing cards under the bed covers with a flashlight after nine o'clock lights-out at night. There I acquired some skill with Gin Rummy.

There were some memorable school occasions and outings in the life of the school. In the fall we occasionally had a half day off to harvest the potatoes and other produce on the school farm. In the spring we took time off to go on a long hike (or ride if we preferred) for an overnight at Raven Rocks some miles away. I remember two occasions in four years when the Ohio River at Wheeling, West Virginia (30 miles away) flooded over its banks, and the boys at school were loaded into the school truck and private cars to go see the flooding. Unfortunately, the girls were not allowed to go along.

One of the things I came to appreciate most in later years, though not so much at the time, was the requirement that we dress up for the evening meals. Seats were assigned at the tables (with a changed schedule every six weeks) so that boys and girls were mixed and paired off. Boys were supposed to seat the girls to their right. The superintendent and matron sat at the head table and tapped a bell when we were to sit down, and again when silent thanksgiving was ended. A teacher sat at the head of each small table of six or eight. We were taught to observe table manners and politely ask for things to be passed, rather than reaching halfway down the table for an extra slice of bread, for example. When I am in homes today where such manners are not observed, I cringe a bit and wish everyone might have had my Friends Boarding School experience. So even though life at the Boarding School was sometimes Spartan and restrictive, I have always been thankful for many of the disciplines I learned there.

One summer during my time at FBS, I wanted to speak to a concern in our Ohio Yearly Meeting business session. Normally young people did not speak to business, so their views were seldom heard in the proceedings. Ohio Yearly Meeting— like other Conservative yearly meetings—had a long-standing Juvenile Committee to oversee and advise about reading material for children. My concern was that the name "juvenile" was a judgmental label for children. Nobody had thought about that, I guess, because that had been the name of the committee for years. So, at the end of that committee's report during yearly meeting session, I addressed the clerk for permission to speak. I stood up and said that I thought the name of the committee should be changed because the pejorative kind of name was demeaning to children and young people.

Well, it caused some discussion. I do not even remember what they did; I think they probably took it under advisement or something like that just to placate me. Anyway, that was a little indicative of my forthcoming demeanor at an early age. It was not my custom to speak in my home meeting as I did there, so it showed something of my occasional boldness. I am sure my family was probably embarrassed, but they never said anything to me.

I was not a very good student at FBS, because I did not take my studies seriously. I was more interested in the girls and trying to be accepted by the other students. These traits sometimes meant some close calls.

One Seventh Day afternoon, I went with three or four other boys from the school to a skating rink in Cadiz, Ohio. I do not think I had ever been on roller skates before. I did pretty well for a beginner. I was whipping around the rink, and I kept passing a boy who was skating with a girl. I kept looking at that girl every time I went by, and he got mad at me for looking at his girl. He finally came over and said that if I didn't stop looking at his gal he was going to punch me in the nose. Well, I did exercise my pacifist upbringing, and I did not talk back. In fact, I backed off. I came awfully close to getting punched in the nose, and the incident soured the whole day for me.

I had a little bit of adventurous spirit in me, in spite of being kept on a leash most of the time. In 1937, during my high school years, my father bought a new Model A Ford pickup truck. That was a great thing for me. We had had a lot of second-hand Model T Fords or Model As. I loved to drive on numerous trips to Youngstown on business. One day, just to see how fast it would go, I got it up to ninety miles an hour going down hill. I didn't keep it there; I just wanted to see if it would do it.

Many important changes have taken place at the Boarding School since my student years. Its curriculum and student life have been broadened to include the educational needs of today's students. Even before these changes were made, FBS was a good learning experience for me. I became acquainted with children from other Quaker backgrounds and traditions from various parts of the United States. As I recall, the school back then did not accept non-Friends. We had some good teachers, and some not so good.

In spite of its limitations educationally, Friends Boarding School was a very important influence in my life and in the lives of many other students who attended. During my time there we had more than eighty students. The majority came from families with a Conservative Friends background, or at least had some connection with such families. Students from the other branches of Friends were also beginning to attend. This was different from student enrollment in later years, when Conservative Friends in the school were outnumbered by non-Conservative Friends and a significant number of non-Friends.

One of the strongest influences I felt at FBS was a genuine sense of community. Although the quality of instruction varied greatly among the teachers, we had a close relationship with them and with the administrators. The school nurtured us with a simple life style and a sense of values consistent with the Quaker founders and benefactors of the school. During my student years it was indeed a yearly meeting school, and I believe it was largely the school that held our Conservative Friends together.

No one would have dreamed back then of the possible demise of the school as has been threatened in recent years because of low enrollment and constant financial difficulties. Of course the student cultural revolution in the 1960s and since has affected the lives of young people at Olney, as it has students elsewhere. This has brought many additional problems in terms of discipline, school values, and practices that had not plagued the school in its earlier years.

If it were not for Olney Friends School, the number of Conservative Friends, especially in Ohio Yearly Meeting, would have declined much more rapidly than it has. Although there has been a steady drop in membership, the Friends Boarding School has helped stabilize the yearly meeting and has given a sense of purpose to those who have rallied to its support. Although, there is something sacred for Conservative Friends about gathering in the Stillwater Meetinghouse for yearly meeting every year, there is something additionally sacred about Olney Friends School which keeps most yearly meeting friends loyal to the school and its traditions.

In the spring of 1999, Olney Friends School underwent a major development that resulted in plans to open the school under new management in the fall. After months of negotiation, Ohio Yearly Meeting Fiduciary Trustees agreed to lease the school—its buildings and grounds—to Friends of Olney, Inc. A new board of trustees was formed and new administration was appointed. Olney Friends School will continue as a Quaker secondary school with support from Olney alumni/ae and Friends of Olney.

One summer day during my Friends Boarding School years, my mother and I had a heavy conversation about my life and behavior. She finally said to me, "Wilmer, all that is wrong with thee is that thee needs to be washed in the blood of the Lamb." Although I had a vague sense of what she was talking about, in my mind I became defensive and asked her to explain what she meant by that. Because she seemed unable to give me a convincing answer, I became defiant, and our conversation came to an unsatisfactory ending.

In subsequent years I looked back upon that incident as turning point in my life, but not in the way she had hoped. Even though I probably knew, and learned more definitively later, that she was talking about the atoning blood of Jesus to cleanse me from my sin and waywardness, it was the beginning of a long religious search that finally ended in my pursuit of a theological education and a Ph.D. degree in theology! That verbal exchange with my mother marked my determination not to accept, willy-nilly, unexamined faith in the theological assumptions and beliefs imparted by my Conservative Friends upbringing. In fact, it was also my declaration that I was ready to examine and test the very ground of my Christian Quaker faith itself.

Chapter Four

Called Beyond the 'Hedge'

L ate in my Friends Boarding School years at Barnesville, I realized that something beyond my Ohio Conservative Friends experience was beckoning me. Because I had no money to go to college, and because my family was not supportive of the idea anyway, I stayed out of school for one year (1938-39) to earn money and to get my bearings on where I was going. I lived at home and worked in the Rural Supply Store, which by then was owned by my cousin Samuel Cooper and my brother James.

The most important thing that happened that year was what I now look back upon as a religious experience involving a conversion. My life turned from where it had been going to a much more intentional life, undergirded with a sense of direction and divine purpose.

I still remember vividly the time and place—a winter First Day afternoon in the boiler room of our greenhouse. The boiler was keeping the hot-house tomatoes and spring vegetable plants warm. I was standing (or perhaps sitting) over the boiler in a nice warm place, meditating and praying about what I was going to do with my life. Suddenly, I had a very strong sense of call that I was to go to college the next year and that I was to prepare for some important work and service ahead. The details of that service were not at all clear at that point.

In subsequent years I came to believe that I had had a religious calling as understood from a Christian and Quaker perspective. It was a calling that stayed with me through the years and carried me through some very difficult times, as well as some very challenging and meaningful experiences. I do not recall that I shared this religious experience with anyone, and I did not understand, then or really for years, what I was going to accomplish.

To follow up my new sense of direction I began exploring various colleges by writing letters for catalogs and consulting with anyone I could about how I might get a college education. I had very little encouragement from anyone, including my Friends Boarding School teachers, or especially from my parents or my Conservative Friends meeting and community.

My Latin teacher at boarding school had told me at the end of my Latin class that she would pass me with a "D" grade but would not be able to recommend me for college. As for my home community, boys of my background were supposed to stay in the community after high school, to help their parents, and try to find employment.

The only person who showed any real interest in my idea of going to college and had much hope for me was my Aunt Lida Blackburn. My mother's sister, she lived in Salem, Ohio, and was well known as a practical nurse. She made it possible for me to have an interview with the Salem High School principal, who counseled with me about seeking a college education.

One specific idea I got for financing my start to college

came from my father's market gardening journal (the name of which I have now forgotten), which told about a man who successfully raised cantaloupe and earned one thousand dollars an acre profit at harvest time. That sounded just right! Given my family's experience in market gardening I felt well qualified to rent an acre of land on the west side of Middleton and begin plans to start the cantaloupe from seed in our greenhouse.

My objective was to raise an acre of melons to sell in time to harvest before college would begin the next fall. It was a great idea, but it turned out to be a fiasco. The acre of cantaloupe was planted and looked fine as the melons began to grow. I arose early in the mornings to dust the melons to control the insects and cultivate the ground for weed control. But the main problem was that I had planted too late in the season for the fruit to mature fully before frost.

Although I harvested and sold some of the crop before Ninth Month, a majority of the nicely forming melons were overtaken by an early frost. Therefore, most of my profit from the sales I made had to go to pay for the fertilizer and land rent. It was indeed a sad conclusion to my great idea to save a thousand dollars for college! My father, although very opposed to my going to college, took pity on me and paid me fifteen dollars for what he thought he could salvage from the crop after the frost was over.

The result of my college inquiries was that I focused on Wilmington College in Wilmington, Ohio. My Friends Boarding School friend, Lloyd Bailey, who was three years older than I, had gone to Wilmington and recommended it to me. In the spring of 1939 my former grade school friend Ed Kirk (the one who tried to convince me that Santa Claus was for real) agreed to go with me to visit the school.

To my surprise I was interviewed by President Walter Collins. He sized me up and finally said words to this effect: "You are a student who is serious beyond your years." I guess he thought I hadn't had much fun in life, was pretty reserved, and maybe was a little too straight-laced—at least compared with most college students. I have never decided whether Dr. Collins intended his statement to be a compliment or whether he was just reacting to a naive nineteen-year-old seeking admission to Wilmington College.

In any event, I was not only accepted for the following September but received a work grant from the Roosevelt Administration's National Recovery Act. I was assigned to the county agriculture agent, Walter Bluck, at the Clinton County Court House in Wilmington. I helped him in his office for a couple of hours every afternoon, except when I had science labs at the college.

Although this work enabled me to meet my main expenses to the college, it was not enough to live on. My Aunt Lida Blackburn loaned me either $100 or $150 to start, with a few similar loans later. So even though my financial brainstorm for college had basically failed, it seemed that "the way did open" for me to go to college after all.

Leaving home in September, 1939, was a tearful experience. My father was so opposed to my going that he did not show up to bid me farewell! My mother was more sympathetic, but she felt it was probably not of the Lord's doing that I go to college. Others of my family stood around in tears, while my boyhood friend Ray Stanley and I took off with my trunk in the back of our Model A Ford pickup truck. (He would return the truck to my home after delivering me to Wilmington College, 265 miles away.) But as I had during the experience at Fairfield Public School when I was in the fifth grade, I was feeling brave and determined that I was going to succeed with this bold new venture, virtually the first of its kind in our Middleton Friends community.

The community was very critical of me when I left. They thought I should stay there. That's what you were supposed to do. Get a bit of education, come back to work in the community, and take care of your parents in their old age. I had a hankering for something more. I felt sadness at leaving, but I knew that the time had come.

I never heard my father say that if you go to college you go to hell, but I know he believed people went to hell, and that it is a pretty bad place. I think he really thought that was where people went if they got involved in higher education. My leaving for college was probably the end of his son's way into heaven, in his terms. My father did not abandon me. We sent letters back and forth, but he must have felt that I was a lost son.

Of course, college opened up a new world for me, entirely foreign to my previous experience. The unprogrammed campus meeting didn't exist when I was there, so I went downtown to Wilmington Friends Church. Ward Applegate was the pastor. It was my first introduction to pastoral Friends. There was no silence such as there is in some pastoral meetings now, but I came to know lots of people and to appreciate that church. In fact, Emily and I were later married there.

Although Wilmington College was not fully accredited in those days, it had several very able teachers. I majored in history with Dr. Willis Hall, who originally came from Quaker City near Barnesville, Ohio, and had been a member of Ohio Yearly Meeting (Conservative). A victim of polio, he walked with crutches and often required someone to help him with transportation. He took a special interest in me, and I earned spare money driving him in the college car to teach extension courses for the college.

Another special teacher was Dr. Frank Hazard, who taught biology. In his classes and labs I first learned about the evolutionary development of life, which, of course, ran counter to my literalistic upbringing on the Genesis account of creation. From then until now, I have never understood why this evolutionary view of God's handiwork isn't considered more miraculous than the creationist view that God brought the world into being in six working days and then rested on the seventh!

Because my primary reason for going to college was to get an education, I did not spend a lot of time in extracurricular activities. I was somewhat shocked to find that Wilmington College had fraternities and sororities, which most students joined primarily because they intended to have a good time while getting their education. Serious and intentional student that I was, I began to look for alternatives to joining the Greek organizations.

The main option was to become active in the YMCA and YWCA student organizations on campus. One of the important "Y" activities involved Gospel Teams that went to outlying Quaker meetings and other churches to lead worship services with spoken messages and music offerings. Since I had no gift for music, I decided to devote my efforts to preparing meditations and sermons. That, of course, also ran contrary to my upbringing among Conservative unprogrammed Friends. That was the way I learned to do public speaking. By my senior year I became chairman of the Gospel Team of twenty-five to thirty students who traveled as teams to one or more appointments, sometimes weekly, usually on Sunday mornings or evenings. My college yearbook for 1947 pictured me behind the pulpit flanked on both sides by a couple dozen Gospel Team members. Had my family known about this activity on my part, they would have been both surprised and distressed.

At the end of the first semester at Wilmington I ran out of money and packed up my trunk to return home. When I went to the business office to turn in my dormitory key, the business manager was completely surprised. He had thought I was fooling him when I had given him fair warning that I was going to run out of money by mid-year. He scurried around and found some scholarship assistance that enabled me to stay in school.

In my second year I hit a more serious stumbling block. The United States Selective Service System was starting to draft men for military service in preparation for World War II, which our country had not yet officially entered. Because I was a Quaker conscientious objector to military service and was backed by several influential Quakers in the Wilmington community, the local draft board classified me 4-E (C.O. status) and on November 7, 1941, shipped me off to Civilian Public Service Camp #19 at Buck Creek, North Carolina. The draft board seemed eager to get me out of town because they apparently feared that my C.O. stand would influence other young Quakers in Clinton County.

My next four years were spent in "work of national importance" in four different CPS camps and units, all of which were under the auspices of the American Friends Service Committee. At Buck Creek we were working for the National Park Service, building Crabtree Meadows Park on the Blue Ridge Parkway. We also fought forest fires up and down the Parkway on emergency calls.

While we didn't have a lot of choice about our placement in CPS camps, I did gain some valuable experience, especially at an AFSC camp in Trenton, North Dakota (CPS #94). We were to open the camp for dry land reclamation and development, and to install an irrigation system to serve the local farmers. There, at age 23, I held my first administrative job—as Assistant Director of the camp of approximately 200 men.

I served under two camp directors, Tom Potts of Philadelphia, and then Ed Peacock, originally from Richmond, Indiana. I enjoyed administration from the word "go." Even though there were hard things to deal with, I seemed able to stay on top of the job.

Early in 1944, I transferred from Trenton, North Dakota, to Philadelphia for most of my last year-and-a-half in CPS. I had requested an assignment at Byberry State Mental Hospital (CPS # 49), partly to get that experience and also because it made it possible to further my college degree. At Byberry (a hospital of over six thousand patients) I worked most of the time on the night shift, so that I could attend classes at Temple University during the day.

Byberry was a very difficult place to work, but it was a very important experience in my life. Part of my time there I worked on the violent ward, and that was very frightening. Schizophrenics would threaten us, and many had to be strapped to their beds. It often took two or three attendants to give a patient a shower. We had very little training, but the administration was glad to have us. Most of their employees had been drafted or were working in industry on the war effort.

After my discharge from Civilian Public Service, I decided to return to Wilmington College in February, 1946, to complete the degree I began there in 1939. With some credit transferred from Temple University in Philadelphia, I was able to finish in a year and a half.

Most important of all upon my return to Wilmington College was meeting my future wife, Emily Haines. During a tour of the campus on my first day back, President Arthur Watson introduced me to Emily, the college dietitian. Wow, what good fortune, even though she was embarrassed to have her just-washed hair wrapped in a towel.

Emily was a very attractive young Quaker woman who had recently graduated as a home economics major from Earlham College. Her home was a Clinton County farm ten miles east of Wilmington near Sabina, Ohio. It did not take us too many months to decide that we wanted to join our lives together in marriage. I think people wondered why this thing was going so fast, when I'd had so much trouble deciding about other girls.

We had a Quaker wedding in the Wilmington Friends Meetinghouse, on December 21, 1946. Ward Applegate, the pastor, did pronounce us man and wife to fulfill legal regulations in Ohio. Other than that it was a Quaker wedding in a Friends meeting for worship. Emily's cousin, a gifted singer, sang the Lord's Prayer. We said our own vows, and witnesses signed the wedding certificate. This was the first time many of the attenders had witnessed such a marriage or had even been in any unprogrammed meeting.

My family came in their "plain Quaker" dress. I think it was difficult for them; it was the first time our families had met. The picture of Emily's and my families at the wedding is one of the few pictures I have of my parents. We are a pretty sober bunch in that picture; none of us look like it's a very exciting occasion!

Marriage always requires adjustments on everyone's part. For instance, in the Conservative Quaker tradition, we didn't wear jewelry. So, I didn't buy Emily an engagement ring; that was hard for her to accept. In fact, I was so in the groove that I wasn't even sure about wedding rings. I had changed enough, however, that I finally decided I would give Emily a ring at the wedding—but I didn't want one myself. After we were married, I did agree to have a ring. I've worn it ever since.

In Emily's family, I also found traditions that certainly were new to me. At home, of course, we had not had any particular celebration around the birth of Jesus and the death and resurrection of Jesus. Even Friends School didn't have a Christmas holiday break. We had a little break, but I didn't know why—except that the new year was coming up. Emily's family had holiday traditions. I had to make compromises, which was hard on my Quaker integrity.

My years at Wilmington College were good ones. It was a culture shock to have collegial relationships with teachers and administrators. I thrived on these relationships, since I knew that many in my Conservative culture weren't very happy with what I was doing.

President Watson always took a great deal of interest in me. He and his wife never had any children, so they often had students in their home more than they would have otherwise. He not only introduced me to Emily, he saw that I had jobs to support myself at Wilmington, helped me get into Haverford College with a T. Wistar Brown Fellowship, and later invited me to teach summer school at Friends University when he was president there. In fact, Emily and I lived for a time with the Watsons in their home in Wichita.

Professor Willis Hall was a remarkable man at Wilmington College. Although he didn't maintain ties with the Conservative Friends community, we shared that connection. As disabled as he was, he not only traveled widely in southwestern Ohio teaching classes, but had traveled all over Europe during his student days. He was always pushing me. We came back to visit him one time when I was working on my

Ph.D. at Vanderbilt University. Professor Hall said, "I think that today, some people are getting two Ph.D.s." Emily about blew her top. She had stuck with me through one, and that was going to be enough!

The summer before I began my studies at Haverford College in 1947, I was asked to serve as Acting Secretary of the Five Years Meeting Peace Board, which involved traveling to most of the nine Friends yearly meetings of the Five Years Meeting of Friends. Emily joined me on most of these journeys from our home base on Quaker Hill in Richmond, Indiana.

This appointment was my first opportunity to become acquainted with the Orthodox/Gurneyite tradition of American Quakerism (mostly pastoral Friends), which made up the Five Years Meeting of Friends (later renamed Friends United Meeting in 1966). That summer experience served me well when I later tried to help two other Friends organizations—the Friends Committee on National Legislation and the Earlham School of Religion—relate to grass roots Quakerism.

My experience at Haverford was a very important time in my development, because I was challenged by the academic rigor of the college. Although I was disappointed that Douglas Steere was on leave that year, Glenn Gray and Martin Foss (a refugee from Nazi Germany) were able professors in the philosophy department. Two very special persons were William ("Uncle Billy") Comfort, the former president of Haverford who taught my Quakerism class, and the very remarkable Rufus M. Jones.

That school year (1947-48) was the last year of Rufus Jones' life. During his forty years of teaching at Haverford, he had built up the highly respected philosophy department. I had several contacts with him in his home, on campus, and at College Meeting. Emily and I were present at Haverford Meeting the last time he attended and spoke. Rufus Jones was very Christ-centered in a liberal way, but in his last message he did not speak about Christ; he spoke about Socrates. It was a memorable message. That Sunday afternoon he had a stroke which resulted in his death a few weeks later.

Just two weeks before Rufus Jones died, I had an important conversation with him about Quakerism as he was sitting up in bed and reading proofs of his last book, *A Call to What Is Vital*. Jones believed that Quakers had their roots in the Continental mystics, who go all the way back to the neo-Platonic tradition that came down through the Catholic Church. I asked him about Geoffrey Nuttall's book that had just been published, *The Holy Spirit in Puritan Faith and Experience* (1947), in which Nuttall gave quite a different interpretation by tracing a strong Puritan influence on Quakerism. (Nuttall, an ordained Congregationalist minister, was a historian of Puritans. He also was familiar with Quakers, because his wife was a Quaker and he attended Quaker meeting from time to time.)

All the historians I knew were taking Nuttall's book quite seriously; in fact, it was one of the turning points for Friends historical interpretations. Rufus Jones had read Nuttall's book, but he said it was too late for him to change his own interpretation at that point.

I completed the masters of arts degree in philosophy and graduated in 1948. My thesis was "The Ethical Implications of Quaker Participation in Politics." During our year there Emily worked for the American Friends Service Committee in downtown Philadelphia. There she started the first AFSC lunchroom cafeteria, which served meals to the staff at noontime five days a week.

From Haverford and Philadelphia we moved in the summer of 1948 to New Haven, Connecticut, where Emily served as dietitian for a junior high school of 1,200 students, while I studied at Yale Divinity School for the next three years. Yale Divinity School was an extremely broadening experience for me as my first major ecumenical encounter with Christians from many different denominations and traditions. At the divinity school I specialized in Christian Ethics and Social Ethics. Some of my most respected professors were Richard Niebuhr, Roland Bainton, and Robert Calhoun.

Because Friends historically did not believe in theological education, and Conservative Friends in particular disapproved of studying for the ministry (though my aim was more directed toward teaching), I never revealed to my family back home what I was doing at Yale University. My father died while I was there in 1950, the same year our first daughter, Suzanne, was born in the New Haven Hospital in July.

If my parents had known that I was studying theology at Yale, I felt it would unnecessarily alienate me from them and the rest of my family. So although I always communicated by letter, I never fully disclosed what I was doing in graduate school, or what my long-term plans were. Neither did my parents and family have much idea or understanding of what I had been doing earlier at Haverford College, or would do later at Vanderbilt University, where I worked for my doctorate in theology.

During my time at Yale Divinity School I had two brief teaching experiences on the side. My Mennonite classmate Gordon Kaufman and I secured part time teaching experience at the New Haven State Teachers' College. Gordon and Dorothy Kaufman became close friends of ours. Gordon and I struggled to hold on to our concern for the peace testimony against the challenge of the strong Niebuhrian nonpacifist influence at the divinity school. We four, and a Baptist couple of similar persuasion, met in one of our apartments nearly every Friday night to eat, play cards and carry on a rather sophisticated discussion about how to defend our peace testimony theologically and ethically. Our wives' tolerance was strained by the conversation, though we made some lifelong friendships in the process. Gordon has since distinguished himself as an author and professor of theology at Vanderbilt Divinity School, and later at Harvard Divinity School.

After receiving my bachelor's of divinity from Yale University in 1951, Emily and I moved to Nashville, Tennessee, where I was awarded the Carré Fellowship to study for the Ph.D. in theology. By this time we had purchased a 1936 Chevrolet sedan to move our things, and to travel back to Ohio occasionally to visit our families. This was the first car we owned in our married life. I had purchased it at Columbiana, Ohio, when I went to my father's funeral in May, 1950, the year before I was graduated from Yale. On our way to Ohio and Tennessee in 1951, we were so short of money that we drove on old U. S. Route 30 through the mountains of Pennsylvania because we didn't have enough cash to pay the toll on the newly opened Pennsylvania Turnpike.

Once we were located in a garage apartment in Nashville, Emily became employed again as dietitian in the doctors' cafeteria at the Vanderbilt University Medical School. We now had our first child, Suzanne, to care for. For a time my sister, Sara Cooper, lived with us.

Like most of my graduate school experiences, these were good years for me educationally, but they were difficult years for our family when Emily had to work to keep us solvent financially. Through it all she carried her end of family and home responsibilities with a lot of grace and very little complaint.

During my studies at Vanderbilt, I took a seminar on John Calvin, which focused on his two-volume *Institutes of the Christian Religion.* I had always been influenced by the Quaker view that Quakers had very little to do with Calvinist or Puritan beliefs. Perhaps some of us were Puritan in our behavior, but in terms of theology we differed with Calvin's doctrine of predestination and election, and his view of human "depravity." (My father grew up in Philadelphia Yearly Meeting [Arch Street] and had nothing good to say about the Hicksite [Race Street] tradition. I sometimes have said my father thought there was one thing worse than Elias Hicks, and that was the devil. And for some Friends the parallel seemed to be that there was one thing worse than the devil, and that was John Calvin.)

The difference between Calvin and George Fox was that though Fox believed in the sinfulness of human nature (although some modern Friends do not believe that he did), he didn't believe that humans were beyond redemption. Fox held that the grace and power of God was sufficient to enable us to overcome our sinfulness. Calvin believed that we are preordained, which leaves little room for human freedom. Quakers have always regarded themselves as closer to the Arminian antithesis of Calvinism and Puritan thought, namely that we *do* have the free will to respond for—or against—God's transforming power and the remaking of our lives.

One of the things I learned in the seminar that really surprised me was Calvin's interpretation of human "depravity." It is not that we are of no value, but rather that in relationship to the greatness, goodness, and glory of God, human beings do not measure up very well. We always seem predisposed to do what we ought not to do, and then we feel guilty about it. *That* was what Calvin meant by "depravity," not that we're worthless sinners. This misunderstanding is why Quakers have felt that Calvin was somebody with whom we don't have anything in common.

Liberal Quakers have gone in just the opposite direction. We believe so much in the goodness of human beings—"that of God in everyone"—that you can use the Seed or Light metaphor, fan that a little bit, and reach up toward God. Another insight I gained from that seminar is an additional reason why I believe that Quakers are rooted in Puritanism, reaching all the way back to Calvin. True, there are many references in Fox's *Journal* to "that of God in everyone," or similar derivations thereof, but what we have overlooked is Fox's constant reference (on almost every page) to the fact that the "power of God is over all." Everywhere Fox went, with every person he met, in every meeting he attended, he felt "the power of the Lord was over all." This "power of God" theme in Fox is a constant reminder of Calvin's belief in the greatness, goodness, and majesty of God. In this respect Quakers were radical Puritans who didn't believe in depravity or predestination, but believed that sin could be overcome and that redemption is possible. Thus we have a responsibility as human beings to decide whether we want to live in accord with God's will for us, or defy God at our own peril.

I finished my residence work at Vanderbilt in 1952 but returned again in 1955 to work on my doctoral dissertation. My subject was "Rufus M. Jones and the Quaker View of the Nature of Man." Some of the research had to be done at Haverford College. During 1955-56 I finished writing the thesis during my recovery from a back operation, which may have been a blessing in disguise. In the early spring of 1956 I took my first plane ride—from Washington, D.C. to Nashville—to successfully defend my doctoral thesis before the theology faculty at Vanderbilt. My reasonably good performance in defending the thesis was due to the fact I knew more about my subject, the Quaker Rufus M. Jones, than did any of my professors!

As the years went by, my sense of Divine leading seemed clear, but the details seemed yet to be fully developed. This sense of an undefined goal continued with me throughout my graduate school years. This was in spite of the fact I assumed all along I would probably become a teacher of religion. The fact that I didn't know the details of my calling was troublesome, not so much to me as to my in-laws.

Emily seemed supportive, though she must have wondered where I was headed, especially when times were difficult financially and she had to provide most of our income. Her parents, especially her father, were hard-working farm folk who believed that a man needed to work with his hands in order to fulfill his responsibilities as a husband and family man. How could one continue as a perennial student, as I seemed to be, and ever fulfill that responsibility? To pursue the advanced degrees I was seeking seemed like a dead end if one could not say precisely how such an education was to be used.

So what *was* my vision that seemed so clear to me but not equally clear to others? I was clear that my future was to be identified with the Religious Society of Friends. That was my spiritual home, and I believed and cared deeply for the Friends message and mission in the world. I was deeply concerned about the divisions within the Religious Society of Friends and longed for greater Quaker unity. I have always believed in building good ecumenical relations with other churches and religious groups, and I believe that we can only be helpful with this process if we know who we are as Friends and have clarity about our own message and mission.

My long-term commitment to this vision was the source of my spiritual motivation. I believed then, and believe now, that God has a very special purpose for the Religious Society of Friends to fulfill in the world.

Walter and Anna Blackburn Cooper's home, Wilmer Cooper's boyhood home (Middleton, Ohio)

Wilmer Cooper, age 6

Walter and Anna Blackburn Cooper

Children in Locust Knoll Friends School (1927–28) Front (from left): Edward Kirk, Alfred Carter, James Edgerton (hidden), William Cope, Charles Carter, and Wilmer Cooper. Back (from left): Albert Binns, Mary Esther Binns, T. Glenn Rockwell, Florence Kirk, Ernest Cope, Helen Cope, Alfred Cope, and Robert Kirk.

Locust Knoll Friends Schoolhouse at Middleton, Ohio.

Middleton Friends Meetinghouse (Built circa 1852; use discontinued December, 1959. Photographed 9/20/1953 at sesquicentennial observance of the founding of Middleton Monthly Meeting, Ohio Yearly Meeting Conservative.)

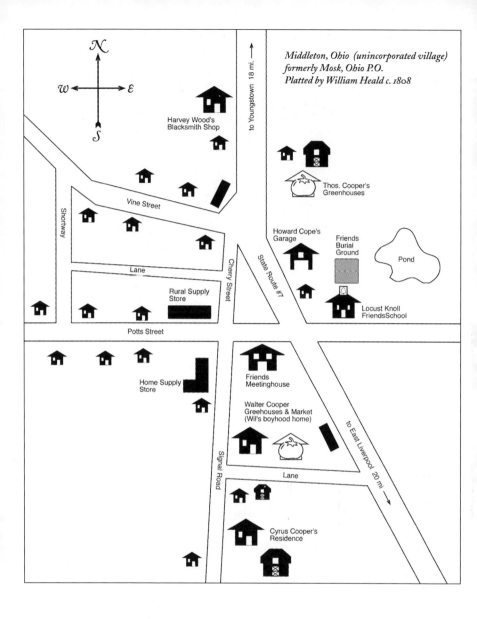

Map of Middleton, Ohio (Line drawing adapted from the Middleton, Ohio Messenger, *Sixth Month 1, 1929, a periodical published and distributed by Cyrus Cooper.)*

Middleton today is different. The meetinghouse still stands but is not used. A new one was built on the west side of the village. Some new businesses have come in; the old blacksmith shop is gone, as well as all the Cooper greenhouses and roadside market. All the streets and roads are now hard-surfaced. My home place is being renovated by my nephew, Walt Cooper, who with his son Wynn have a thriving auto body shop and used card dealership.

Class of 1938 Friends Boarding School, Barnesville, Ohio. First row (from left): Jean Anne Rife, Walter Hartley, Ruth Peacock, Joseph Taber, Ruth Binns, Naomi Hartley. Second row: Lorena Pemberton, Merle Pickett, Frances Guindon, Edward Kirk, Anna Marie Henderson, Leslie Thomas, and Harriet Starr. Third row: Cameron Satterthwaite, Charlotte Carpenter, Wilmer Cooper, Alice Hoag, Robert Hartley, and Eleanor Hoge.

Wilmer Cooper (FBS years).

Gathering of Conservative Friends, March 20-22, 1997, Olney Friends Boarding School

LEFT: *Aerial view of Olney Friends Boarding School campus. Main Building is left center; Stillwater Meetinghouse, top right.*

ABOVE: *Main Building, Olney Friends Boarding School (1920s).*
LEFT: *Stillwater Friends/Ohio Yearly Meetinghouse, Barnesville, Ohio.*

Friends walking path from Olney Friends School to Stillwater Meetinghouse. Wilmer Cooper's Uncle Cyrus Cooper fourth from left (light gray hat).

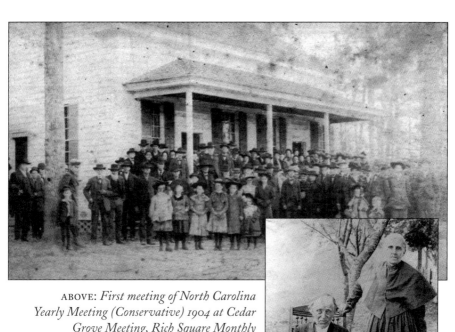

ABOVE: *First meeting of North Carolina Yearly Meeting (Conservative) 1904 at Cedar Grove Meeting, Rich Square Monthly Meeting, Woodland, N.C.*
RIGHT: *Thomas and Mary Barker Hinshaw, founding members of Holly Spring Meeting, North Carolina Yearly Meeting Conservative (est. 1910, Friendsville)*
BELOW RIGHT: *Anna C. Fisher in 1940s typical plain dress. Recorded minister, one-time clerk of NCYM Conservative.*

Elwood and Phebe Conrad, members of West Grove Monthly Meeting (est. 1912) NCYM Conservative. At right: Benjamin P. Brown, minister. Member of Rich Square Monthly Meeting (Cedar Grove at Woodland) taken at the home of John Norwood.

Hickory Grove Meetinghouse, between West Branch and Springdale, Iowa (Scattergood School in distance). Insert: Close up of Friends Boarding School "known as Scattergood Seminary" in West Branch, Iowa from postcard dated 1908.

Paullina (Iowa) Mapleside Friends Meeting (Iowa Yearly Meeting Conservative) 1910 with schoolhouse.

IYMC in Earlham, Iowa before meetinghouse was moved to Bear Creek.

Levi Bowles (ca. 1940) In 1937, Wilmer Cooper drove his Uncle Cyrus Cooper to IYM (Conservative) at Paullina. "Levi Bowles was the first to speak in open worship. I never forgot it."

ABOVE: *Jenkins House, Earlham School of Religion 1968. Original administrative and faculty offices.*
RIGHT: *Alexander Purdy (left) was Wilmer Cooper's mentor in his early years as Dean of ESR.*

Wilmer and Emily Cooper at Wil's retirement, 1985.

Chapter Five

The Vision
Made Real

From Nashville we moved to Washington, D.C. in the summer of 1952 as I began work with the Friends Committee on National Legislation on Capitol Hill. Sam Levering, a North Carolina Friend who had been chair of the Five Years Meeting Peace Board when I worked with it, recommended me for the position. There were various reasons that persuaded me to take the job.

Although I had been thinking in terms of a teaching position through my years at Haverford, Yale, and Vanderbilt, the work at FCNL gave me an opportunity to live into some of the questions I had posed in my master's thesis at Haverford on ethical issues for Quakers in politics. I also felt that, as a Conscientious Objector, it would be a good idea if more Quakers showed that the other side of taking advantage of our C.O. privilege was offering ourselves in peace time service for a period after the war. I had decided that if the chance came to serve in some way, I would do so before I found a position at a Quaker college.

The Friends Committee on National Legislation had been established by a committee of Friends from all over the country who met in Richmond, Indiana, in the summer of 1943. By that time, the American Friends Service Committee was realizing that much of the advocacy work it was doing had political implications. The leadership feared they might endanger the AFSC's tax-exempt status if the organization got too involved in trying to influence legislation in Washington. They suggested a separate agency that would not be tax exempt to lobby without apology for what it wanted to advocate. The group that met in Richmond concluded that Quakers should have a special representation in Washington, so they formed FCNL. E. Raymond Wilson, who did not attend the meeting in Richmond but had been on the staff of AFSC, was asked to head up the new organization.

I came in during the tenth anniversary of FCNL. In fact, about the first thing I did was to organize a series of tenth anniversary celebrations all over the country. These were dinners that Raymond and I attended with the intention of raising $1,000 at each dinner. That was a lot of money in those days. We succeeded in most cases.

My work on Capitol Hill with FCNL, as a colleague of Raymond Wilson's and with a dedicated staff, was a very rewarding experience. It broadened my understanding of the political process and allowed me to express my concerns for peace and justice in the social and political sphere. Although I was registered with Congress as a lobbyist for FCNL, most of my time was spent as Administrative Secretary of the Committee. This meant overseeing the staff of fifteen or so, raising funds from the Quaker constituency, and traveling widely among Friends to interpret the work of the Committee.

One of the rewarding aspects of my work at FCNL was that I discovered again that administrative work was one of my gifts. Even though being away from home a lot was difficult, I really knew I was interested in working with Quakers, and I was able to get acquainted with them at the grass roots level. In the course of my travels I had the good fortune of discovering Edward F. Snyder of New York Yearly Meeting, who became legislative secretary for FCNL in 1955. He later replaced Raymond Wilson as executive secretary. Near the end of my time in Washington, one of my accomplishments was the relocation of the FCNL offices from 104 C St., N. E. to a new location up the street at 245 Second Street N. E., adjacent to the new Senate Office Building.

Again these were good years, but also difficult ones. Two of our four children were born at the George Washington Hospital during our seven years in Washington—Cathy in 1953 and Barbara in 1955. I always had a guilty conscience—as more men ought to have today—about being away from home so much in my work and leaving Emily to raise the children without me. She likes to talk about that, and I'm still trying to do penance. I give her the credit for all the good things that our children grew up to be, and I take some responsibility for any of the problems.

We became very attached to our Garrett Park, Maryland, community where we lived outside of Washington. It was from this quiet, friendly and attractive suburban town that I rode the B & O train every day into Union Station in Washington, a ten-minute walk to my work at FCNL on Capitol Hill. It was also in Union Station, in fact, where Landrum Bolling, then president of Earlham College, first talked to me about making a long-time Quaker dream come true.

There had long been a vision of establishing a Friends training school for ministry under the auspices of what had become the Five Years Meeting of Friends in 1902. In my book, *The ESR Story: A Quaker Dream Come True* (1985), I give an account of several of these efforts to realize this vision through the years. In 1957, under the auspices of the Five Years Meeting of Friends, a National Conference on Ministerial Training was held at Germantown, Ohio. Most of those concerned with the idea of a ministerial school were present, including several from Earlham College; I had come from Washington, DC. But it was not until 1958, when Landrum Bolling became the new president of Earlham College, that a plan was developed to make a study of the possibility of establishing such a school at Earlham.

I received a call early that year from Landrum Bolling saying that he was going to be in Washington and asking me to meet him at Union Station between trains. In that meeting, we talked for maybe forty-five minutes or so about the feasibility study, and he invited me to come to Richmond for an interview on campus that fall in November, 1958.

These were exploratory discussions, but it was pretty clear that Landrum was determined during his administration to see if he couldn't do something about this recurrent dream of a Quaker seminary. Five Years Meeting would have liked to launch it themselves, but there was no way they had the kind of funding that a college is able to draw. And so it was reasonable for Earlham to try. Several of the Quaker colleges—Friends University, William Penn, and Guilford—had tried to start such a program earlier. Landrum Bolling invited me to come to Earlham to head a survey on the school and to determine support among Friends for it.

Our move to Earlham from FCNL in the summer of 1959 was the beginning of the fulfillment of my vision and sense of calling that came to me in my "conversion experience" in 1938-39. We moved to Earlham with what some would call "blind faith" that the dream of a Friends school for the ministry would come to fruition. To demonstrate our faith we contracted for the building of a house near the college in Richmond.

Since a full account of this story is told in *The ESR Story*, I will only recount the basic facts about how the Earlham School of Religion came into being in 1960. I arrived at Earlham on April 1, 1959, to begin a six-month survey and feasibility study for the establishment of a Friends school for the ministry. We sold our house in Garrett Park and moved into a new house at 300 S. W. "H" Street in Richmond in July of that year, halfway through the feasibility study.

In the autumn, after traveling fifteen thousand miles and writing a seventy-page feasibility report to President Bolling and the Earlham Board of Trustees, I was asked to join the faculty of Earlham College's Religion Department. This allowed for some lead time so that those concerned with the project could study my report and make up their minds about establishing a graduate school of religion at Earlham. By the fall of 1960 we were authorized by the board to continue the Earlham College M. A. in religion for two years, with the possibility of adding the three-year bachelor of divinity degree (now called either master of divinity or master of ministry).

The formal decision to establish the Earlham School of Religion was not an easy one for the Earlham College Board of Trustees. There was concern about the size of the task itself, about whether ESR would draw income away from the college, and about whether the seminary would match the high level of academic standards of the college. The board spent a major part of their February, 1962 meeting making a decision.

One new trustee in particular tried to stop approval over a period of several months. The board met all day Friday and late into Friday evening, and still couldn't make a decision. Howard Mills, chairman of the board, decided to hold the matter overnight. The meeting began on Saturday with a quiet time. At the opening of business, Howard Mills said: "My head says we can't do it, but my heart says we have to." All the other board members quickly approved. The new trustee had stayed away from that meeting because he had felt that was what would probably happen.

I was named dean of the Earlham School of Religion when the board of trustees approved the development of the school in 1962. I knew when this happened that this was what I had been led toward all my life. My earlier sense of call had given me an assurance of purpose for my life. And even though I didn't know just what I was preparing for, I just followed this call as I felt led.

There were many hard times in the beginning of the ESR, including some internal friction between Earlham College and ESR. Many Earlham faculty thought that the kind of Quakerism in Indiana and Western Yearly Meetings was going to fail in the end and wondered what we were doing trying to save it. ESR received full accreditation by the American Association of Theological Schools of United States and Canada in 1975, although it had enjoyed associate membership since 1968. Today, and in recent years, there has been strong support for ESR both from Earlham College Presidents Richard Wood and Douglas C. Bennett, as well as from the Earlham College Board of Trustees.

Alexander Purdy was an important influence in the first five years of ESR and was my mentor in the early years of my deanship. A professor of Bible and religion at Earlham before going to Hartford Theological Seminary, Alexander Purdy served for forty years as professor of New Testament and eventually dean of the seminary. More than one hundred Quaker pastors were trained at Hartford under the tutelage of Alex and his colleague, Moses Bailey.

Purdy was a highly respected Quaker both here and

abroad, having served as chairman of the Friends World Committee for Consultation, Section of the Americas. Upon his retirement from Hartford Seminary, we persuaded Alex to join our faculty in the fall of 1960 as Professor of Biblical Studies. He came planning to stay for one year and stayed five.

As a startup seminary we encountered many difficulties both externally and internally. I felt we should try to get a good cross section of Friends on our faculty, including representation from Evangelical Friends. In all my years at ESR, we did not succeed as well as I had hoped. One of the most testing times when I was Dean—the only time I was ever ready to throw in the towel—was a particularly difficult fundraising campaign in 1966-67.

ESR had hired a respected company from New York to run a campaign for $1.3 million. Lilly Foundation had made a $300,000 challenge gift based on our raising $1 million from Friends. (In those days, no one thought it was possible to raise a million dollars from Quakers.) By October 1967 we had raised $600,000; at that point the professional fundraising organization declared that the million-dollar goal couldn't be reached and it pulled out of the campaign.

Only strong encouragement by former Earlham College President Tom Jones, a first-rate fundraiser himself, kept me on track. He gave me a "dressing down" for even thinking of giving up: "We're not going to give up; we're going to succeed."

Delbert Replogle, chair of the Earlham School of Religion Board of Advisors, called a meeting at the Cincinnati airport of some of the weightiest members of the board—Willard Ware, Oscar Marshburn, Bernard White, Marcus Kendall, along with a couple of visitors, and our Earlham staff: Landrum Bolling, Tom Jones, Leonard Hall, and myself. Everyone was committed to claiming that $300,000 from Lilly Foundation, even though we only had until the end of the year to meet the million-dollar goal. Three board members said we should re-start the campaign on our own. They pledged to make up the difference if we didn't reach the goal. We carried out their wishes and met the goal without having to call on their pledges.

In October 1960, our family was enlarged with the ar-rival of our first son, Timothy Scott Cooper. These were in-deed busy years for Emily, especially when I was appointed Dean of ESR. We did the usual amount of entertaining in our home that a head-of-school does, including student and fam-ily groups, graduating seniors, and visiting Friends and digni-taries.

In 1968, after that strenuous but successful financial cam-paign, I was granted a six-month sabbatical leave. This coin-cided with my appointment as Friends United Meeting's rep-resentative to the World Council of Churches and my first trip abroad in that capacity. Although Emily and I had been to Ireland for the Friends World Committee for Consultation Triennial in 1964, we decided this time to include our four children in a family trip to Europe in the summer and autumn of 1968.

We left in June for Luxembourg, where a new Volkswagen camper van was waiting for us. We drove ten thousand miles through eight countries in Western Europe, Scandinavia, and the British Isles. In our travels we attended London Yearly Meeting and took the Quaker tour to northwest England be-fore settling down for three months at Woodbrooke, the Quaker study center in Birmingham, England. Our children, ages eight to eighteen, were enrolled in local schools, except for one who flew home to attend Friends Boarding School. We returned to Richmond in time for Christmas.

Administration, fundraising, traveling, and speaking—along with part time teaching in theology, ethics and Quaker studies—filled my days as dean at ESR until 1978 when I left that position to remain on the teaching faculty. My official retirement at age sixty-five came in 1985, though I continued to teach Quaker studies for another five years. Since retirement I have served ex-officio on the ESR Board of Advisors and kept in touch with ESR, supervising several independent studies for students.

When I was asked by Landrum Bolling to head up the Earlham School of Religion, some people wondered how on earth they could ask me to be dean of a school in the business of training pastors when I had never been a pastor myself. I had a lot of convincing to do.

I enjoyed teaching at ESR, even though my administrative duties limited my time in the classroom. I was a good teacher, not great. No matter what the subject, I encouraged expression of all opinions. In fact, some of the best grades went to students who disagreed with me. I still keep in touch with some former students, and I value those connections. All teachers have students for whom we are an important influence.

After publication of *The ESR Story* in 1985, I began work on another book. Five years later Friends United Press published *A Living Faith: An Historical Study of Quaker Beliefs*. This book has met with a very positive response and is now in its fourth printing. It has become a standard text for Quakerism classes and Quaker study groups and has been translated into at least one foreign language.

By the mid-1970s, when our children were mostly grown up, Emily entered graduate school herself at Ball State University in Muncie, Indiana, and took an M. A. degree in home economics in preparation for employment as a Women, Infants and Children (WIC) nutritionist coordinator. This job was part of a federally supported program that provides supplementary nutrition support for low-income pregnant mothers, infants, and children up to age five. She opened the program's first clinic in Wayne County, Indiana, in 1979 and later expanded it to a three-county area in east central Indiana serving approximately twenty-five hundred clients. Because of the success of the program nationally it is one of the few agencies which has survived the Federal welfare cuts. Emily officially retired as WIC Coordinator in 1990, but continued working part time for a couple more years in the agency.

At the time of Emily's retirement from WIC, she proposed the idea of a Mentor Mothers program and worked with several other women and the YWCA to get it started. The program links first-time mothers with more experienced women who serve as mentors for child rearing and responsible motherhood.

Emily is very much of a people person, who derives great satisfaction doing helpful things for others. She is much more down to earth and practical about meeting human need than I am. Her success as a dietitian, her ministry to the needs of children and their moms through WIC, her vision for a Mentor Mothers program, and her kindness to others in the community all testify to her gifts with people.

As I reflect on my thirty-one years with Earlham College and ESR, I realize that I had great hopes and expectations for the ESR's preparation of persons for ministry and service in the Religious Society of Friends. Although not all my hopes have been fulfilled, ESR has made a significant contribution by providing leadership for Friends and the wider church. Today ESR is no longer an experiment; it is an important educational center serving primarily North American Friends.

The 1994 coming of Bethany Theological Seminary (Church of the Brethren) to join ESR in a cooperative venture in theological education has added strength to both schools. Because both belong to the Historic Peace Church tradition, they complement each other in many important ways; yet each school is able to maintain its separate identity and commitment to its respective religious and church constituency. Only history will be able to tell the full story of ESR's significance and its lasting impact.

My life and work have been shaped by three forces—my growing up in one of the strictest families among Ohio Conservative Friends, my awakening to a sense of direction in my life the year after I was graduated from Friends Boarding School, and my interest in the interaction of religion and politics.

I know that my family influenced my life direction. In part, I felt that if I went into the field of religion and into religious service of some kind, I could get some approval from them. I think my mother and father both became more accepting of me before they died, but they were never really happy that I did what I did.

I do have a deeply religious side to my life. I studied various forms of spirituality and wrote my doctoral thesis on Rufus Jones, the one who introduced mysticism so thoroughly to Friends. I have had some mystical experiences, but I do not put a lot of stock in mysticism as such. I think it is indeed a form of spirituality that some people find deeply meaningful. Even though Rufus Jones wished everybody would have this experience, he was not sure everybody did.

I believe that you really can be led by the Holy Spirit, by the Christ within, or by God in your life. My mother was spiritually attentive even to the very small things, not just big issues. Day to day, hour by hour, she was moving in the Spirit of the Lord. I had always bought into that idea, and I still believe it, although I don't practice it as well as I should. I try to be attentive, still, to spiritual leadings. The most difficult thing, as anyone knows, is to discern the real leading of the Holy Spirit. Our leadings need to be continually checked with others. When we do not do that, we get ourselves in trouble. But, of course, a primary purpose of the Quaker meeting is to be a community of persons to help us discern the truth in our leadings. I'm thoroughly a Quaker in that sense.

My interest in politics led to an interest in political philosophy. Because I was interested in philosophy and religion, I became interested in ethical questions: How do ethics apply to the political situation? Is there room for Quakers—in an effort to live out their testimonies on peace and equality, for example— to engage in political activity? These questions formed the basis for my master's thesis at Haverford, "The Ethical Implications of Quaker Participation in Politics."

My work with FCNL, of course, gave me the opportunity to apply religion to politics. Some of my early writings are in this area. In Washington, I also learned a lot about how politics work in getting things done. (Few Quakers will admit the amount of politics in Quaker practice.) I do not regard politics as a bad or evil thing; I see the political process as a fundamental need that can be good or bad.

My doctoral thesis was related to these issues, because I believe that all political philosophies are ultimately shaped by one's view of human nature. For example, the famous philosopher Thomas Hobbes' pungent assertion that "the life of man [is] solitary, poor, nasty, brutish and short" represents a kind of pessimism that goes too far in the other direction. In other words, any view of human proneness to sin and evil has important political ramifications.

For my Ph.D. thesis at Vanderbilt, therefore, I decided to study Rufus Jones' view of human nature and how that has affected our Quaker view of the political and social order. My title was: "Rufus M. Jones and the Quaker View of the Nature of Man." I selected Rufus Jones because he unquestionably has been the most influential Quaker for the twentieth century, even though I have not always agreed with him. Indeed, I concluded that on this issue he helped to mold Quaker thinking into an unduly optimistic view of human nature, and therefore of life in general. Such optimism easily falls prey to a superficiality that verges on naiveté about sin and evil as part of the human condition. I believe there *is* a valid Quaker optimism that is based not on our own strength and ingenuity but on our faith in a God whose grace and power is great enough to enable us to personally and corporately rise about our own human limitations. A life lived in harmony with God's purposes *can* effect extraordinary human accomplishment in this life, and thus provide the basis for authentic hope for humankind and for the future.

Richard Niebuhr, brother of the theologian Reinhold Niebuhr, was one of my mentors at Yale Divinity School. Both of these men had a profound influence on my thinking, so much so that I have been referred to as the "Niebuhrized Quaker." The Niebuhrs' political philosophy, which emphasized personal and corporate sin in public life, helped to temper my Quaker optimism. This, coupled with my Conservative cultural upbringing, caused me to challenge some of Jones' easy assumptions about the human condition and our role in shaping history.

I still follow very closely what's going on in Washington, D.C. and around the world. I listen to two or more news programs regularly and keep myself informed on current events. I am also still keenly interested in the ethics of politics and trying to relate religion and politics. Given the tremendous political crisis in Washington, D.C. as I write in 1998, I find the application of religion and ethics to politics increasingly difficult, but I believe it essential to the survival of civilization.

Today I am struggling philosophically about the question of separation of church and state. There is a long tradition among Christians, especially Baptists, for the separation of church and state; there used to be no crossing over. But through FCNL Quakers *do* cross over; we try to apply our religious principles to the political life of the country. This has always seemed to me the right thing to do, yet when Jerry Falwell and Pat Robertson (and a whole host of others) try to apply *their* religion to politics, they come out at an entirely different place than I do. Maybe separation of church and state is a time-honored tradition in America that we need to take seriously, though not to the divorce of ethics from our political life.

I probably have too many academic degrees. I don't know how I kept getting scholarships through my undergraduate and graduate years; I was smart enough, but not the smartest. Nels Ferré, my major theology professor at Vanderbilt, claimed that you could accomplish almost anything with the right motivation. Perhaps I was blessed with discipline and motivation because of my sense of calling and Divine leading early in my career. I was convinced I was preparing for something important. However, I always wished I'd been a little *smarter.* Given my strong motivation, I might have accomplished even more.

Upon my official retirement from Earlham School of Religion in 1985, I was awarded an honorary doctor of divinity degree from Earlham College. In my response to the awarding of the degree, I said I wished that two persons could have been present to witness the occasion. One was my Friends Boarding School Latin teacher who passed me with a "D" grade in Latin but said she could not recommend me for college. The other was my father who distrusted higher education and tended to believe that if you went to college you probably would go to hell. Had he lived to witness my achievements as the result of my college and university education, I don't know whether he would have modified his views about the uncertainty of his son's eternal destiny. Because he had only an eighth grade education, it was hard for him to think beyond his own limited experience. And because he believed in a literal hell, it is just as well that he never lived to witness my lifetime involvement in higher education, and in particular, theological education.

Also at the time of my retirement, ESR launched a fundraising campaign to endow Cooper scholarships to promising Quaker students who would be nominated by their monthly meetings. These would cover full tuition for a stated portion of their preparation at ESR for leadership in the Religious Society of Friends. A quarter of a million dollars was raised for these Cooper Scholarships in recognition of the work Emily Cooper and I did in establishing the Earlham School of Religion. Five or more such scholarships have been given each year since the program was established in 1985.

As this book goes to press yet another honor has come my way—this time from my *alma mater*. At its fall, 1998, alumni gathering in New Haven, Connecticut, I was awarded Yale Divinity School's Award of Distinction for Theological Education for my role as founding dean of ESR in 1960. When I received the news about the honor, I was taken by surprise. The next day I wondered if I had imagined it all. However, when Emily told our cleaning woman that I was to receive this award at Yale Divinity School, she asked, "What's that?" Her momentary response has helped me to gain a better perspective on the importance of such an honor!

I get more accolades than I deserve for what I did at ESR, but I did bring an understanding of the importance of attending to details and a clear sense that I was fulfilling a calling. I also have a lot of stick-to-it-iveness and patience. Other persons who came after me had other gifts, but I think I was the right person to get the school started.

I had no idea I would ever be so fortunate as to be the founding dean of ESR. Many things just fell in place. Things do not just fall in place for many people. I feel sad about that, and I don't know why they can't get their sense of direction. I was given my sense of direction on that First Day afternoon long ago in the Cooper Greenhouse boiler room—and I am grateful for it.

The Vision Made Real

Chapter Six

A Plea for
the Future

As I look back upon Conservative Friends of the mid-twentieth century, many memories and impressions come to mind. Some of these have to do with Friends customs and standards of behavior, which often seem strange and foreign in today's world. In the early days Friends were referred to as "a peculiar people," a term which they themselves accepted as a sign of a transformed life. This meant bearing some distinctive marks in obedience to one's Christian and Quaker calling. It meant a heightened quality of one's spiritual life in character, demeanor, dress, and address. When called upon, it meant bearing one's cross and witnessing to one's faith publicly. This was considered to be one's religious duty—even to the point of deprivation and suffering, if need be, for conscience's sake and obedience to Divine leading.

Being labeled as "a peculiar people" was often misunderstood even by one's closest neighbors and acquaintances in the community. A humorous illustration of this is told by Sylvester Jones out of his Quaker past in Kansas around the turn of the century. Similar stories could be told about other Friends meetings on the American frontier. It shows how isolated and set apart Friends were in their own communities, which caused others to misunderstand them:

> On First Day and Fourth Day we were taken to meeting. At first it was in the old oblong meeting house situated some miles away, with its facing benches of the gallery.

A story which had its setting in this meeting house at Tonganoxie is told by a Mr. Cadwalader, whose name betrays his Quaker ancestry but whose ignorance of Quakers gives point to the story as he told it. "I have always had Quakers for neighbors," he said; "They have been mighty good neighbors. But I have noticed one peculiar thing about them. Every Wednesday morning just before eleven o'clock, no matter what they were doing, they would leave it and go over to the meeting house and stay there about an hour. I often wondered what they did there. Now it occurred to me that there was no reason why I shouldn't go over some Wednesday morning and find out. They are my friends and neighbors. Why not go to Quaker meeting? So one Wednesday I quit my work and went. The Quakers were standing around talking about weather and crops and such things. Suddenly just at eleven o'clock Uncle Jesse Blair got spunky about something and went up on the facing bench and sat down and began to pout. Then all the others as if seized by a common impulse scattered out over the room and began to pout. They sat there and pouted for about an hour. Finally Uncle Jesse Blair got ashamed of himself and reached over and shook hands with the one nearest him. Then they shook hands all over the room and made up and began to talk about the weather and the crops and things just like other folks."[1]

It is difficult to know whether friend Cadwalader really experienced Quaker silent worship as pouting or whether the hour was so lacking in deep spiritual worship that he did not experience anything about it. As a boy in our "silent" Friends meeting, I recall that some of the most refreshing times of worship occurred when not a word was spoken. Those were the times we corporately experienced the living presence and transforming power of Christ in our midst. This happened most often at our midweek meeting on Fifth Day morning, whereas on First Day public ministry was common and expected.

My memories out of the past also bring some troubling recollections. Things were not always peaceful in the Quaker fold. Given their strong witness for peace and reconciliation, why were Friends not always able to apply these principles to themselves? Differences appeared which led to splits in monthly, quarterly and yearly meetings. Strict enforcement of the Book of Discipline by the elders and overseers was the cause of some Friends being disowned from their monthly meetings. These things happened in my home meeting, which caused much pain for everyone. In one case an entire family (including the grandfather, his two sons, and their families) were disowned after several years of a "power struggle" between that family and the rest of the monthly meeting.

Kenneth Morse, a Conservative Friend from Ohio Yearly Meeting, in 1962 published *A Short History of Conservative Friends*, which enumerates a number of these cases and the disciplinary action that was taken. Kenneth researched three meetings that he believed to be representative of Conservative Friends in the latter part of the nineteenth and early part of the twentieth centuries. He found that out of a total of 1,131 disownments in these three meetings, 46 percent were for "going out in marriage" (i.e. disowned for marrying a non-Friend out of meeting), 25 percent for sexual immorality, 5 percent for drunkenness, 4 percent for disobeying the peace testimony, and 2 percent for dancing. Then he adds, "Contrary to a seemingly current belief, I found no one disowned for failure to use the plain language or failure to dress plainly...."[2]

Morse then made a more detailed study of the Somerset Meeting of Ohio Yearly Meeting, 1820-1869. From this he reported the following: 142 disowned for "going out in marriage"; 118 disowned for joining Hicksite Friends between 1828-1844; 18 for joining the Methodists; and 11 for unchastity and fornication.[3] In 1829 Somerset Meeting disowned a member "for dancing, attending places of diversion and deviating from the truth...."[4] The author also quotes Eliza H. Varney, a convinced Friend from Ontario, Canada: "How deeply I regret to see young people going to theatres and dancing halls when they might have true enjoyment at home. Life is too brief to waste in amusements that lead away from Christ and win us to the world."[5] There were a number of cases reported in which there had been a violation of the Discipline, but those involved were reinstated in membership when they did recompense for their misdeeds and asked for forgiveness.

Friends Boarding School maintained similar standards. For example, in 1884 baseball was forbidden "chiefly because of its association with gambling and other vices."[6] But change was on the way. By 1928 the school no longer required girls to wear bonnets, and boys were allowed to wear plain-cut collars on their coats—but not a notched collar, which was regarded as too fancy. And for the first time Christmas vacation was allowed for the students, a sign that Conservative Friends were beginning to observe the "day which the world calls Christmas."[7]

Change was also taking place in other meetings of Ohio Yearly Meeting. In the 1920s and '30s Friends primary schools (located next door to their meetinghouses) were being discontinued for lack of students and financial support. In 1944 Salem Quarterly Meeting for the first time held joint sessions of men and women, abandoning the practice of separate seating for men and women on two sides of a meetinghouse partition. By 1950 Ohio Yearly Meeting had followed the same practice. The early custom was that some people knelt to pray while others in the congregation stood. By 1962 this custom was beginning to give way: some people stood to pray while others in the congregation remained seated. In ministry, the old practice of sing-song or intoned chanting during public ministry was noticeably disappearing. All of these changing customs were symptomatic of the gradual relaxing of the Discipline and its puritanical standards of behavior.

Another area of Quaker concern, especially among Conservative Friends, was the customs and standards that related to the Quaker testimony of simplicity. Even though for Friends the inward dimension of life takes precedent over outward display, nevertheless consistency between the two must be maintained, and a single ethical standard is the goal. This standard was deeply rooted in the example of Jesus and the Sermon on the Mount. Conservative Friends in particular did not feel they should be encumbered with the outward demands and fashions of their day. This meant that simple living was their objective. But some compromise has always been inevitable even though they sought consistency in their behavior.

In today's world Friends are repeatedly challenged by the new technology and materialism that constantly bombard us. It has become increasingly difficult, if not impossible, to avoid both the advantages and disadvantages which the new technology offers. At times technology seems to consume us even though there are other times when it helps to simplify our lives. Friends and others who are immersed in this way of life are constantly looking for ways to be consistent with the Quaker testimony of simplicity in daily living.

In 1966 the Center for Plain Living sponsored a gathering called "The Second Luddite Congress," with support from the Foundation for Deep Ecology. Friends of Ohio Yearly Meeting granted permission for the conference to take place in their yearly meeting house at Barnesville. The gathering considered the impact of modern technology on our personal, family and community lives and how limiting the use of technology may help in shaping a more wholesome lifestyle. There were some 350 in attendance, some from the "plain people" tradition, including Friends, as well as others who are seeking a simple life "back to the land," and a number coming from deep involvement in the complexities of modern technology. Although those who gathered gave different reasons for their plain and simplified style of life, some disagreed about how pure they should try to be as compared with those who were willing to accept some compromise as inevitable. Still others believed that joining together in community is the best way to deal with the dilemma of living the simple life in a very complex world.[8]

What this adds up to is that faithfulness to the Conservative Friends tradition has grown steadily more difficult. Life is more complicated, and the temptations of conformity have increased manyfold as compared with a generation or two ago. To be a purist or an absolutist in these matters is increasingly difficult, if not impossible, from a human perspective.

Growing up among Conservative Friends, I had a thorough grounding in their historic beliefs and testimonies. I came to know them experientially and not just from hearsay or out of books. I was not always convinced of the Conservative Friends interpretation of their beliefs and testimonies, partly because of the discomfort they caused me in my growing up years. But my Conservative Quaker upbringing did have a positive impact on me in many ways that have remained throughout my life.

I benefited from a moral and religious education unlike most other children received. I had instilled in me a sense of integrity for daily living, which for the most part was sound and has served me well. Even though I have had some regrets for the way I was shaped by Conservative Friends and about the way in which I responded to that influence upon me, I have much for which to be thankful. This is especially true when I observe the very difficult issues and problems facing parents in the proper nurture of their youth today.

As we look at the future of Conservative Friends we have to decide whether they are a relic out of the past to be treated as a curiosity, or whether they represent potential for new life and growth in the future. In Iowa and North Carolina Yearly Meetings (Conservative), some of the new life today resembles Friends General Conference Quakerism more than traditional Conservative Friends beliefs. Similarities with FGC tend to place them in the liberal Hicksite tradition more than the Conservative Orthodox tradition from which they sprang. Part of the reason for this is that many newcomers to these yearly meetings have found their way into the Religious Society of Friends through the American Friends Service Committee and the peace movement without fully realizing that Quakerism is first of all a religious movement and a spiritually motivated way of life. It is only secondarily a force for social service and change. The two should not be seen in conflict, but neither should one be emphasized at the expense of the other.

Another quality that seems to be emerging among liberals seeking membership with Friends is a hunger for a Quakerism as a non-Christian form of spirituality, with less emphasis on social activism. But whatever the reasons are for becoming a Friend, authentic Quakerism should fully integrate both the inward and outward as an expression of what Friends call the sacramental view of life. Friends believe that every occasion and event can serve as a channel for God's grace, and that such occasions and events can serve to unite us sacramentally with God and the living Christ within.

Ohio Yearly Meeting, somewhat in contrast to North Carolina and Iowa, is regarded by many as the remaining yearly meeting most rooted in the customs and tradition of Conservative Friends. But Ohio Conservative Friends have not been clear about their own identity. They have been exposed to developments from within and without which have not always been consistent with Conservative Wilburite Quakerism. From within there have been three different responses to these developments:

1. There have been those in Ohio Yearly Meeting who have yearned for new life and vitality but sought it by association with Holiness Christian groups, or by way of the charismatic movement. The result has often produced confusion rather than clarity as to what Conservative Friends stand for.

2. There is a handful of Friends in each of the three Conservative Yearly Meetings who cling tenaciously to past tradition with the determination to preserve what they believe to be authentic orthodox Quakerism.

3. A more recent response, especially in Ohio Yearly Meeting, has been a small group of newcomers who have been deeply impressed by the dignity, simplicity and integrity of Conservative Friends to which they feel drawn like a magnet. For them this kind of Quakerism has been a new and liberating discovery. Some of these persons have delved deeply into the history of Quakerism and believe that Conservative Friends best embody the insights of the early Quaker vision. They believe Conservative Quakerism could become like a spring in the desert for many seekers who feel lost and disillusioned by

the religious confusion they experience in the world about them, as well as for other branches of the Religious Society of Friends itself.

Membership in all three Conservative Friends yearly meetings has declined over the years, though springs of new life keep emerging. For several years there has been an informal General Meeting of Conservative Friends and fellow travelers held intermittently at various locations. The last in 1995 in Barnesville, Ohio, drew more than a hundred people who came from near and far, including England. An unusual number came who have adopted the plain dress and customs of their Conservative forebears. Some seem drawn because they are "seekers after the truth" and are finding new meaning for their lives among Conservative Friends.

Many of the historic Conservative Friends beliefs and practices cited earlier are acknowledged and claimed today by Friends in the three Conservative yearly meetings, while others do not feel connected with the Quaker past as there described. There are some who are in full accord with the historic Christ-centeredness of Conservative Friends, together with their time-honored practice of "waiting upon the Lord" in worship and ministry.

Similarly, the atoning work of Christ described by early Friends and retained by Conservative Friends into the twentieth century has alienated some but remained essential for others. Howard Brinton has dealt helpfully with the debate over this and related doctrinal issues by differentiating between the Wilburite and Gurneyite Friends in the nineteenth century:

> The differences between Wilburite and Gurneyite was [sic] not superficial. The Wilburites emphasized right experience as essential to salvation, the Gurneyites right belief.... Though the Wilburites believe in the work of the Christ of history as

essential, their preaching was confined to the necessity for the work of the Inward Christ, who, if yielded to, would transform the Christian into the likeness of Christ. For the Gurneyites, Christ's work of redemption was completed on the cross, and acceptance of that sacrifice was the primary means of salvation. The Wilburites excluded formal Bible teaching, believing that all genuine religious activity must have its origin in the direct, immediate inspiration of the Holy Spirit. Since the Gurneyites laid great emphasis on the Bible as the primary source of right belief, Bible teaching and lectures on religion were for them essential.[9]

Friends have always welcomed "continuing revelation," but it has not been easy to agree on how to relate this to the unique revelation of God in Jesus Christ, and to the continuing work of the Spirit of God now and into the future. Most would say tradition is important, but most would also agree that we should not become hide-bound to tradition. The question is how to take advantage of the past as we move into the future. Openness to new growth is just as important as rootedness in past commitments and achievements.

There are two broad categories of Friends today, "liberal" and "evangelical." Neither term is precise and completely accurate, but they encompass a broad view of the Religious Society of Friends. Friends General Conference (FGC) and a few independent yearly meetings, such as Intermountain, Pacific, and North Pacific, are off-shoots of the liberal Hicksite tradition dating back to the Hicksite/Orthodox separations in 1827-28. Friends United Meeting (FUM, formerly Five Years Meeting of Friends) is an international body of Friends who stand in the Orthodox tradition of the Evangelical Gurney Friends. For the most part they worship in programmed pastoral meetings, whereas FGC Friends worship in unprogrammed meetings, gathering in the silence to wait upon the Spirit. Although there are many unprogrammed meetings in other parts of the world, FGC is confined largely to North America.

Evangelical Friends International (EFI, formerly Evangelical Friends Alliance) also claims its Orthodox Evangelical Gurneyite heritage along with Friends United Meeting, but it does not include any unprogrammed meetings as does FUM in New England, New York, Baltimore and Southeastern Yearly Meetings. Like FUM, EFI is international in scope. It tends to be more conservative and evangelical in theology and church organization than Friends United Meeting. Both EFI and FUM have placed a strong emphasis on missionary work to other cultures and faith traditions, whereas the FGC and related unprogrammed meetings stress service work as their main form of outreach.

The largest growth of Friends in the last century has resulted from Friends missionary work, particularly in Kenya, East Africa (FUM), Central America (EFI), and in some other places in the world. The service work of Friends, especially after the two World Wars, has become worldwide through the efforts of the American Friends Service Committee in Philadelphia, and Quaker Peace and Service in London.

There are significant theological differences between the Hicksite tradition (FGC) and Orthodox Friends (FUM and EFI). The source of religious authority for the Hicksites has been the Inward Light, whereas the Orthodox have emphasized the authority of the Bible and the guidance of the Holy Spirit. The Hicksites have had a Unitarian view of the Godhead, whereas the Orthodox have usually emphasized a traditional Trinitarian approach—God, Christ, and Holy Spirit. The Hicksites were more rationalistic than the Orthodox, who stressed the leading of the Spirit with minimal emphasis upon human reason. The Hicksite de-emphasized sin in human nature, whereas the Orthodox believed all have sinned and need to be redeemed. The Hicksites believed in continuing revelation, while the Orthodox placed special emphasis on the revelation of God in Jesus Christ. These are a few of the theological differences which have been the source of friction and misunderstanding between these two major branches of Friends.

Conservative Wilburite Friends arose out of the Orthodox tradition that separated from the Hicksites in 1827-28, and they constituted the other part of the Gurney/Wilburite separations which took place at mid-century. Conservative Wilburite Friends have held views in sharp contrast to the Hicksites while retaining many of the Orthodox beliefs they had prior to the Gurney-Wilbur Separations. Their small numbers (now around 1,500) are no match for the other branches of Friends.

A new factor in Quakerdom has emerged in the latter part of the twentieth century, namely, the Quaker Universalist movement, which claims that the Christian frame of reference is too limited and restrictive for Friends. They believe that all religious experience points to a source of truth greater than that embodied in any one religion, including Christianity. In the past, there was a universalism acknowledged in the Religious Society of Friends, which was best articulated in Robert Barclay's *Apology*. His basic premise was the universality of the Light of Christ within (the *Logos*), which was personified in Jesus Christ. George Fox and Barclay both claimed that this Light of Christ can be known spiritually by all humankind and was sufficient for salvation whether or not one had heard of the name of Jesus.

This early Quaker Universalist formula is not inclusive enough for the Quaker Universalists of today. As a result they have evolved apart from Friends in the Evangelical, Orthodox, and Conservative Friends traditions (i.e. most of FUM, EFI and Conservative Wilburites). Conservative Friends regard the Christ-centeredness of their faith as a given that is essential to their Quakerism. What little dialogue there has been among Friends about this difference has done little to resolve the issue in the minds of Friends.

Conservative Friends share some common theological views with the evangelical Gurneyite Friends. These include their Christ-centeredness and their reliance upon the Scriptures to confirm inward leadings of the Holy Spirit. But when it comes to the practice of worship and ministry, the Conservative Quaker approach differs from Evangelical Friends. At the same time, much of Evangelical Friends practice is a departure from the Quakerism of the past, and often resembles other Christian denominations.

If the test of authentic Christian Quakerism is to determine who has been consistently loyal to Friends historic faith and practice, then Conservative Wilburite Friends receive high marks. But if such an historic test has little to do with what is authentic Quakerism, then both liberal and evangelical Friends are at liberty to revamp Quaker faith and practice according to their own leadings. Then the question is, against whose standards are those leadings to be tested? Both the "faith stance" of liberal Quakerism and the "practice stance" of evangelical Quakerism are quite unlike historic Quakerism. It is this discrepancy that bothers Conservative Friends in their relationship to the other Friends bodies— FGC, FUM, EFI and the independent yearly meetings.

Friends determine the standards by which they put their faith into practice by what they call "continuing revelation." This is a very important principle of Quakerism. But for Conservative Friends the question has always been: How does continuing revelation relate to the unique and unrepeatable revelation of God in Jesus Christ? To use a British Friends expression, this original revelation for Conservative Friends is the "steadying central conception" of Quakerism. It is a stabilizing standard for judging God's continuing revelation today.

Though Conservative Wilburite Friends sometimes appear to be on the way out, it is surprising how much interest and respect is shown toward them by other Quakers. Some of this may be due to an occasional hankering for the "old ways" of Friends and thankfulness for the fact that a few are still practicing those "old ways." But one discerns something more than respect and a desire to keep alive this Quaker tradition.

There is a sense that maybe these Conservative "plain" Friends (though they are not as plain as they used to be) have been able to retain some values and testimonies which have been lost by more progressive Friends. When I was a boy growing up among these folk, we called these other Friends not only "progressive Friends" but "fast Friends." Is it possible that today's "fast Friends" would really like to slow down a little and recover some of the relative peace and quiet and plainness of the "old ways"?

Of all the distinctive qualities of Conservative Friends, I believe their commitment to integrity is the most important. We talk about Quaker peace and justice testimonies, but I think each of us comes to those in a significant way only if we have a sense of integrity about life—how we treat people, how we conduct our own life.

There have always been some Conservative Friends who feel embarrassed and apologetic about their plainness and simple way of life. Some of them often show their restlessness to become like other Friends and free themselves from their "peculiar" Quaker identity. But my plea is for them to be themselves and not try to be somebody or something they are not. It has been said that a liar is someone who tries to be someone he or she is not. If that is true, then Conservative Friends' sense of integrity calls for them to be who they are. That may be part of their calling and mission to the world as well as to other Friends.

At the Friends Consultation on Diversity and the Future of Friends held at Quaker Hill Conference Center in Richmond, Indiana in 1997, Carole Edgerton Treadway shared an intriguing suggestion for the future role of Conservative Friends in the wider Religious Society of Friends. She asked whether Conservative Friends might become "a bridge between evangelical and liberal Quakerism." To provide some substance for the idea, she pointed out how the Conservative tradition was both similar to and different from these two parts of the Quaker spectrum and said: "I make [this suggestion] with caution, and with more faith and hope than solid experience, given the many influences and strains that exist in Conservative Quakerism and considering that its adherents are too few and too scattered to have much influence." Whether or not this is a viable proposal, it is suggestive of the ways in which Friends in general might become more useful and helpful to each other in becoming a united body with renewed spiritual vitality and vision for the future.

Perhaps the larger question is whether Quakers in general have had their day and are doomed to recede into history. But our basic faith is one of hope and promise for new life in the future. Numerically we are small and not very successful by the world's standards, yet we must be reminded that probably the most significant and influential movement in history was started by God's initiative in the life and work of Jesus Christ and a not too impressive handful of disciples, not all of whom were faithful to Jesus' vision and resurrection promise.

George Fox was captured by this vision and mission when the Religious Society of Friends was born in his day. Why might it not happen again in our day? Perhaps some of the old wineskins will have to be discarded and replaced by new ones to meet the needs of God's work in today's world.

Conservative Quakerism is not doomed to extinction, but based on past performance neither is it likely to experience large growth and become a major segment of the Religious Society of Friends. It can be a living example of a faithful remnant holding high the beliefs and practices of historic Quakerism. Presumably, only God knows and can determine Conservative Quakerism's future as a light on a hill and pattern for the rest of Quakerdom and the wider world.

I have not attempted to answer all the questions that might be asked about Conservative Friends, but to help those who are drawn to Conservative Friends to better understand them and their past, and to encourage an openness to the future. The seventeenth-century English nonconformist John Robinson, who interacted with the Quakers of his day, uttered a relevant word for Friends today: "The Lord has yet more truth and light to break forth from his holy word."

I hope Carolyn Treadway is correct in her thinking that Conservative Friends may serve as a bridge among Friends in the future. Kathryn Damiano experienced that potential as she researched her doctoral thesis: "On Earth as It Is in Heaven: Eighteenth-Century Quakerism as Realized Eschatology."

More simply stated, eighteenth-century Quakerism was a vision "of living a patterned life of faithfulness that was understood as literally bringing the Kingdom of God on earth now." This, Kathryn believes, was what early Friends envisaged in the seventeenth century, what was characteristic of eighteenth-century Quaker Quietism, and what has been the vision of Conservative Friends in the nineteenth and twentieth centuries.

Kathryn reports, "I had many conversations with Elmer Hartley when I 'hung out' with Conservative Friends in Ohio as part of my research (for the dissertation). After quite a few glasses of lemonade and many stories, Elmer asked me if I wanted to know the 'essence of Quakerism.' His answer was 'total reliance on Divine Providence.' That really captured me."

I knew Elmer Hartley when I was growing up. He was a modest and thoughtful person who believed every one of those words—as did many others among the Conservative Friends who nurtured my life. This is not to say that these Friends always fulfilled the commitment to "total reliance on Divine Providence" in their own lives, but they fervently prayed that God would enable them to do so. This commitment, coupled with our commitment to integrity in daily living, also defines the essence of Quakerism today for me. These elements are at the heart of the Christian faith and our Quaker practice thereof.

1. Sylvester Jones, *Not by Might, A Little That Is Never Too Late* (Elgin IL: The Brethren Publishing House), 1942, pp. 9-10.

2. Kenneth S. P. Morse, *A History of Conservative Friends* (Barnesville, Ohio: Published by Kenneth Morse, 1962). See Preface.

3. *Ibid.*, p. 29.

4. *Ibid.*, p. 36.

5. *Ibid.*, p. 49.

6. *Ibid.*, p. 10.

7. *Ibid.*, pp. 10, 12-13.

8. Tom Goodridge, "Struggling With Simplicity: The Second Luddite Congress," *Friends Journal* (August 1996), pp. 16-18.

9. Howard H. Brinton, *Seventy-five Years of Quakerism, 1885-1960,* (Philadelphia: Philadelphia Yearly Meeting of the Religious Society of Friends, 1960), p. 9.

Highlights of a Journey
Wilmer A. Cooper

Editor's Note: In some ways, identifying certain dates and activities thus far in Wilmer A. Cooper's life goes against the belief of early Friends (and many Conservative Friends) that each of our days is holy, and all should be celebrated equally. It is also good spiritual discipline, however, to be mindful of the gifts we have given and have received. We offer the following list of milestones in gratitude for Wil Cooper's intellectual search, faith, and continuing service to the Religious Society of Friends.

April 20, 1920	Born in Middleton, Ohio, the youngest of the five children of Walter M. and Anna Blackburn Cooper.
June, 1938	Was graduated from Friends Boarding School at Barnesville, Ohio.
Winter, 1938-39	Conversion experience gave a sense of call beyond the community of Ohio Conservative Friends.
September, 1939	Entered Wilmington College, Wilmington, Ohio.
November, 1941	Began service as a Conscientious Objector in Civilian Public Service Camps during World War II.

February, 1946   Renewed study at Wilmington College.

December 21, 1946   Married Emily Haines in Wilmington
                        Friends Meeting.

May, 1947   Awarded B.A. in history from Wilmington
                        College.

Summer, 1947   Served as acting secretary of Five Years Meet-
                        ing Peace Board.

1947-48   Entered Haverford College, Haverford,
                        Pennsylvania, as T. Wistar Brown Fellow.
                        Awarded M.A. in philosophy in May, 1948.

1948-1951   Entered Yale Divinity School at New Ha-
                        ven, Connecticut. Awarded bachelor of di-
                        vinity degree in 1951.

July 25, 1950   Daughter Suzanne Cooper born in New
                        Haven, Connecticut.

Fall, 1951   Entered Vanderbilt University in Nashville,
                        Tennessee, as Carré Fellow. Awarded Ph.D.
                        in theology in 1956.

1952-59   Served as administrative secretary of Friends
                        Committee on National Legislation (FCNL)
                        in Washington, D.C.

May 25, 1953   Daughter Cathy (Cooper) Papazian born in
                        Washington, D.C.

June 22, 1955   Daughter Barbara (Cooper) Bartl born in
                        Washington, D.C.

Summer, 1957	Helped establish Quaker Theological Discussion Group, which met annually and publishes a journal, *Quaker Religious Thought*.
July 1, 1959	Moved with Emily and Suzanne to Richmond, Indiana, to begin feasibility study at Earlham College for a training school for Quakers in the full time ministry.
October 24, 1960	Son Timothy Scott Cooper born in Richmond, Indiana.
February, 1962	Named dean of Earlham School of Religion, as Earlham College Board of Trustees formally establishes the seminary. Served as dean through 1978.
1968-1975	Served as Friends United Meeting's representative to the World Council of Churches.
1970-80	Served as chair of an ongoing Quaker Faith and Life Panel.
1980-90	Convened, with Quaker Hill Conference Center, annual Consultations of Friends on Quaker faith and practice issues.
June, 1985	Retired from faculty of Earlham School of Religion. Awarded an honorary Doctor of Divinity Degree. Cooper Scholarships were established in honor of Wilmer and Emily Cooper by Earlham School of Religion. Continued to teach part time until 1990.
June, 1985	*The ESR Story: A Quaker Dream Come True* published by Earlham School of Religion.

June, 1990	*A Living Faith: An Historical Study of Quaker Beliefs* published by Friends United Press, Richmond, Indiana.
May, 1997	Awarded Honorary Doctor of Humane Letters, Wilmington College, Wilmington, Ohio.
November, 1998	Awarded Yale Divinity School's Alumni Award for Distinction in Theological Education.

Appendix A

Conservative Friends Book of Discipline, 1922 edition Ohio Yearly Meeting

In order that the Yearly Meeting may be clearly informed of the state of the Society, the following queries are directed to the subordinate meetings: and, in desiring answers to them, the design of the yearly meeting is, not only to be informed of due observance of the several branches of our Christian testimony, but also to impress on the minds of our members a profitable, individual examination of themselves, how far they act consistently with their religious profession; and also to encourage elders, overseers and other concerned Friends, to discharge their duty faithfully, in administering counsel and admonition when necessary.

It is concluded that the following eight queries be read, deliberately considered, and answered in each Preparative and Monthly Meeting, once in the year, in order to convey an explicit account, in writing, to the Quarterly Meeting next preceding the Yearly Meeting; and from thence an account is to be forwarded to the Yearly Meeting.

Also that the first, second and eighth of those Queries be read and considered, and explicit answers be prepared for them in the two Quarterly Meetings preceding the one before mentioned, and also in the Preparative and Monthly meetings which report thereto. But none of the Queries are to be read or answered in those Quarterly Meetings for Discipline which immediately succeed the Yearly Meetings which report to those Quarters.

And further, it is not obligatory on meetings to read any other of the Queries than such as are to be answered; nor is the reading and answering of them enjoined on any Preparative Meeting where the members of that and the Monthly Meeting are the same.

First Query. Are all meetings for worship and discipline duly attended? Do Friends avoid unbecoming behavior therein? And is the hour for assembling observed?

Second Query. Do Friends maintain love toward each other, as becomes our Christian profession? Are talebearing and detraction discouraged? And, when differences arise, are endeavors used speedily to end them?

Third Query. Are Friends careful to train up their children in the nurture and fear of the Lord? And to restrain them from vice and evil company, and keep them to plainness of speech and apparel? And are they encouraged, frequently, to read the Holy Scriptures?

Fourth Query. Do Friends maintain a faithful testimony against the manufacture or use of intoxicating liquors? Against the attendance of places of unprofitable entertainment or diversions? Do they observe moderation and temperance on all occasions?

Fifth Query. Are the necessities of the poor, and the circumstances of those who may appear likely to require aid, inspected and relieved? Are they advised and assisted in such employment as they are capable of? And is due care taken to promote the school education of their children?

Sixth Query. Do Friends bear a faithful testimony against a stated or paid ministry, oaths, military or naval services, fraudulent business, and against engaging in or encouraging lotteries or gambling of any kind?

Seventh Query. Are Friends careful to live within the bounds of their circumstances, and to avoid involving themselves in business beyond their ability to manage? Are they just in their dealings, and punctual in complying with their engagements? And where any give reasonable grounds for fear in these respects is due care extended to them?

Eighth Query. Is care taken to deal with offenders seasonably and impartially, and to endeavor to evince to those who will not be reclaimed, the spirit of meekness and love, before judgement is placed upon them?

Annual Queries

It is also required that the following Queries be read and answered once in the year, in each Monthly and Quarterly Meeting, and a written report thererof forwarded to the Yearly Meeting by the respective Quarters.

First. What new meetings settled? What meetings discontinued?

Second. Are schools encouraged for the education of our youth, under the tuition of teachers in membership with us?

Third. Are the Queries addressed to the Quarterly, Monthly and Preparative meetings read and answered therein as directed?

General Advices

It is further directed, that in the Preparative and Monthly Meetings in which all the foregoing Queries are read and answered, the following advices may be read, with a suitable pause between them, as a means of inciting those present to a consideration whether there is any occasion for an extension of care in these respects, in relation either to themselves or others.

Friends are advised:

To observe due moderation in the furniture of their houses, and to avoid superfluity in their manner of living.

To attend to the limitations of truth in their temporal business.

To be careful to place their children amongst Friends, preferring those whose care and example will be most likely to conduce to their preservation.

To inspect the state of their temporal affairs once in the year, and make their wills whilst in health.

To apply for certificates when about to remove, and to pay proper attention to those coming from other places, who appear as Friends, without producing certificates.

And it is advised that when occasions of uneasiness appear in any, such may be treated with in privacy and with tenderness before the matter be communicated to another; thus, the hands of those concerned in the further exercise of the discipline, will not be weakened by a consciousness, on their part, of a departure from the true order of the gospel.

It is also recommended that all our meetings for business be kept select, and that Friends endeavor to manage the affairs of Society in the spirit of meekness and wisdom, with decency, forbearance and love to each other; laboring to maintain the "Unity of the spirit in the bond of peace."

And Friends are encouraged to so order and regulate their business, and social affairs, that they harmonize with, and foster spiritual growth; and manifest, in their every day lives, the seasoning influence of the spirit of Christ.

Appendix B

Conservative Friends Book of Discipline, 1992, edition Ohio Yearly Meeting

General Queries and Advices

When these were first instituted, it was the design of the Yearly Meetings to provide a means for maintaining a general oversight of the membership pertaining to our Christian life and conduct. It remains this Yearly Meeting's heartfelt desire that good order and unity may be maintained among us.

To further this purpose, the Yearly Meeting feels that the attention of each member of the Society should be drawn at regular intervals to individual self-examination. To aid the members in the exercise, a series of both Queries and Advices is provided to impress upon the minds of us all various principles and testimonies which should guide our daily lives.

Queries

The following Queries are directed to be read, pondered and answered once in the year in each Monthly and Quarterly Meeting, in a deliberate and unhurried manner. Answers to two of the queries (three in Second Month) are to be forwarded to each Quarterly Meeting, where these queries and answers from each Monthly Meeting are to be read, and a summary report approved. The Quarterly Meeting Clerk then collects these summary reports throughout the year, and forwards the entire group to the Yearly Meeting.

1st Query. Are Meetings for Worship well and punctually attended? Is our behavior therein conducive to meditation and communion with God? Do we maintain a waiting spiritual worship and a free gospel ministry? Do we welcome others to share this fellowship with us?

2nd Query. Do we cherish a forgiving spirit, and strive to "...*Walk in love, as Christ also hath loved us," (Ephesians 5:2)* Is each one of us careful for the reputation of others? Are we ever mindful to love our neighbor as ourselves? If differences threaten to disrupt the Christian harmony between the members, is prompt action taken?

3rd Query. Are our homes places of peace, joy and contentment? Are they an influence for good in the neighborhood, community, and country? Do we set a good Christian example for our children to follow? Are Friends careful that their children realize our loving Savior will faithfully guide them through life, as they are willing to accept and obey him? Do we help our children to read and appreciate the Bible?

4th Query. Believing our bodies to be "...*The temple of God,*" *(I Corinthians 3:16)**, are we concerned to attain a high level of physical and mental health? To this end, are our lives examples of temperance in all things? Do we avoid and discourage the use and handling of intoxicants, tobacco, and improper use of drugs?
*(I Corinthians 6:19, 20 & II Corinthians 6:16)

5th Query. Are we sensitive to the needs of those around us who may be in less fortunate circumstances? Do we prayerfully consider how we can share one another's burdens when the need arises? Do we counsel lovingly and prayerfully with those members whose actions in any phase of life give us grounds for concern?

6th Query. Do we live in the life and power which takes away the occasion of all wars? Do we, on Christian principles, refuse to participate in or to cooperate with the military effort? Do we work actively for peace and the removal of the causes of war? Do we endeavor to cultivate good will, mutual understanding, and equal opportunities for all people?

7th Query. Do we observe simplicity in our manner of living, sincerity in speech, and modesty in apparel? Do we guard against involving ourselves in temporal affairs to the hindrance of spiritual growth? Are we just in our dealings and careful to fulfill our promises? Do we seek to make our Christian faith a part of our daily work?

8th Query. Are we careful to use the affirmation rather than the oath? Do we avoid gambling and speculation based on the principles of chance?

9th Query. Are we sensitive to the problem of family living? Do we offer counseling to couples both before and after marriage? How are we helping individuals, married couples and family units to strengthen and enrich their lives?

Advices

We believe the custom of regularly reading aloud well chosen advices has been of value to our members in stimulating their spiritual life.

It is directed that each of the following Advices be read in our meeting, at least once in the year, according to a regular plan, and that the time for reading them be chosen to benefit as many of the members as possible.

A suggested plan follows: Arrange for someone to read aloud one portion weekly at the close of First-day Meeting for Worship, followed by some minutes of silence in which to consider it. This would allow for the reading of each advice twice in the year.

1. Use vigilant care, dear Friends, not to overlook those promptings of love and truth which you may feel in your heart; for these are the tender leadings of the Spirit of God. Nor should any of us resist God's workings within us, for it is His redemptive love which strives to show us our darkness, and to lead us to true repentance, and to His marvelous light. *"Behold, I stand at the door and knock: If any man hear my voice, and open the door, I will come in to him, and will sup with him, and he with me." (Revelation 3:20).*

2. Be faithful in maintaining your testimony against all war as inconsistent with the spirit and teaching of Christ. Live in the Life and Power that takes away the occasion of all wars and strife. Seek to take your part in the ministry of reconcilia-

tion between individuals, and groups, and nations. Let the law of kindness know no limits. Show a loving consideration for all people.

3. Regard the taking of oaths as contrary to the teachings of Christ, and setting up a double standard of truthfulness; whereas, sincerity and truth should be practiced in all walks of life.

4. In your Meeting for Worship be earnestly concerned to enter reverently into communion with God. Come with minds and hearts prepared. Yield yourselves up to the influence of the Divine Presence so that you may find the evil in you weakening and the good raised up. God calls each one to the service of the meeting. Be obedient and faithful, whether by work or silent prayerful waiting; and be ready to receive the message of the others in tender spirit.

5. Be on your guard, dear Friends, lest the love of pleasure take too strong a hold of you. Choose such recreations as are pure and healthful. Let them be in harmony with your service to God and men; and in that service be ready at any time to lay them aside when called upon.

6. Endeavor to make your home an abiding place of joy and peace where the Presence of God is known and felt. Seek to know an inward retirement, even amid the activities of daily life. Make a quiet place in your daily life, wherein you may learn full meaning of prayer, and the gladness of communion with your Heavenly Father.

7. Avoid and discourage any kind of betting or gambling, as well as commercial speculation of a gambling character. Remember how widespread are the temptations to grow rich at the expense of others, and how apparently harmless indulgence leads, often by degree, to ruin and crime.

8. Watch with Christian tenderness over the opening minds of your children. Help them to understand the teaching

of Jesus. Seek to awaken in them the love of Christ, and through example and training in self control, to bring them to obedience to the law of God in their own hearts, that they may be joyful and willing in His service.

9. In consideration of marriage, remember that happiness depends on a deep and understanding love. Seek to be joined in a common discipleship of Jesus Christ. Ask guidance of God, desiring above all temporal consideration, that your union may be owned and blest of Him. Consider the precious responsibilities of parenthood, and do not forget the help you may draw from the loving counsel of your own parents.

10. Carefully maintain truthfulness and sincerity in your conduct, and encourage the same in your families. In your style of living, in your dress, and in the furniture of your houses, choose what is simple, useful and good.

11. In view of the evils arising from the use of tobacco and intoxicating drinks, we urge all to abstain from using them, from offering them to others, and from having any part in their production, manufacture, or sale. Do not let the claims of "good fellowship" or the fear of seeming peculiar prevent you from standing by principles which you have conscientiously adopted.

12. Members are affectionately reminded of the importance of keeping correct and clear accounts pertaining to all outward affairs. It is important to make or revise wills or living trusts while still in health of mind and body, and free from any feeling of resentment. Delay, or neglect to secure competent legal advice, may cause some unexpected hindrance in the proper execution of one's bequests.

13. Make it your aim to promote the cause of truth and righteousness, and to spread the Kingdom of God at home and abroad. Be ready to take your part fearlessly in declaring His message and in witnessing to His power.

14. Live in love, as Christian brethren, ready to be helpful one to another. Rejoice together in the blessings of life; sympathize with each other in its trials. Know one another as fellow-workers in the things that endure. Watch over one another for good; praying that each may be a living member of the Church of Christ, and may grow in the knowledge of the love of God.

15. Remember the special opportunities for refreshment of spirit and for service which the first day of the week affords; use them faithfully, as befits Friends of the Master.

16. Be diligent in the reading of the Bible and other spiritually helpful writings. Gather daily in your families for worship. Such times have a special value in bringing little children especially into the experience of united worship, and so preparing them for the larger Meeting for Worship, as they learn in the silence to bow to the power of God.

17. Be mindful for yourselves and for your children that you value the beauty and power of good friendships. Also, by example and precept, encourage your children to appreciate the best in literature and the arts, which is consistent with our Christian faith. By this, all your lives may be enriched and the youth with tastes thus early formed may henceforth instinctively choose the beautiful and good.

18. Seek for your children that full development of God's gifts which true education can bring about. Remember that the service to which we are called needs healthy bodies, trained minds, high ideals, and an understanding of the laws and purposes of God. Give your best to the study of the Bible, and the understanding of the Christian faith. Be open-minded, ready constantly to receive new light.

19. Be zealous that education shall be continued throughout life. Willingness to be used in mind as well as in body, and

to be equipped in both, is a needful part of a Christian character. Our service to God is incomplete without the contribution of the intellect.

20. Follow steadfastly after all that is pure and lovely and of good report. Be prayerful. Be watchful. Be humble. Let no failure discourage you. When temptation comes, make it an opportunity to gain new strength by standing fast, that you may enter into that life of gladness and victory to which all are called.

21. A punctual attendance at the hour appointed for Meeting for Worship is a matter of no small importance. If we hurry from outward occupation, we are in danger of two things: Our thoughts may still be with that in which we have been engaged; and our late arrival may interrupt that holy silence which should prevail; however, let us welcome with open hearts all who join us no matter when they arrive.

22. We would urge Friends, when away from home, to attend a Meeting for Worship if such is within reach. Such attendance may well strengthen the meeting, and may bring Friends who were hitherto strangers into fellowship with one another.

23. Those who visit our Meetings for Worship should be given friendly welcome and be encouraged to continue to join us in worship. Particular assistance and loving attention should be accorded new members.

24. When we gather in worship, let us remember that there is committed to us, as disciples of Christ, a share in the priesthood. We should help one another, whether in silence, or through spoken word, or prayer. Let none of us assume that vocal ministry is never to be our part. If the call comes, there should be no quenching of the Spirit. The sense of our own unworthiness must not exempt us from this service, nor must the fear of being unable to find the right words, *"for it shall be*

given to you in that same hour what ye shall speak." (*Matthew 10:19)*

25. We should recognize the importance of finding occasion for some united worship during the week, either at the meetinghouse, or in a private home. Such maybe of great assistance, not only to the individual, but also to the life of the whole group.

26. Let your whole conduct and conversation be worthy of disciples of Christ. *"be ye steadfast, unmovable, always abounding in the work of the Lord."* (*I Corinthians 15:58)*

27. Remember that our spiritual life will not be complete unless we have experienced an inward baptism and transformation. Growth in inward purity and outward Christian effectiveness should follow this experience, but such growth can come only if we persist in seeking to know and follow the commands of Christ.

28. In their senior years, and before debilitating infirmities prevail, Friends are affectionately admonished prayerfully to seek Divine Guidance and counsel from their families and friends regarding plans to continue to live in their own homes, enter a retirement home, or to make other living arrangements appropriate for their financial capabilities in their last years.

Appendix C

A Short History of Conservative Friends

by John Brady

Prelude: Orthodox Friends

The Religious Society of Friends began the nineteenth century as a united body. Apart from some small schisms in the 1600s, and another small secession of non-pacifist "Free Quakers" in the American Revolution, the Society had been, from its early days, remarkably uniform in doctrine and practice. To a great degree, however, outward harmony masked inward spiritual decline. As the first generation of Friends had passed away in the early 1700s, the Society had increasingly become a hereditary group defined less by its faith than by its way of life. The institution of birthright membership produced many nominal members who did not share the experience of convincement that had gathered early Friends. Growing wealth and comfort in the Society inevitably resulted in more worldliness. Both inward devotion and outward adherence to the Discipline were fading.

Ministers and other leaders among Friends had been decrying this trend from at least the mid-1700s. Rather than seeking a renewal of faith within the Society however, the leadership attempted to deal with the problem by tightening enforcement of the Discipline that governed details of Friends' outward conduct. Plainness of dress and speech became the hallmarks of a "consistent" Friend. The plain life, at its best, served to protect the inward and outward life of Friends from corruption by the world's temptations. As one Book of Discipline stated:

> ...this singularity is not without its use. It is in some respects like a hedge about us, which, though it does not make the ground it encloses rich and fruitful, yet it frequently prevents the intrusions by which the labor of the husbandman is injured or destroyed.[1]

Increasingly, however, husbandry of the hedge became the chief work of the Society's leaders. The result was, predictably, a strict but often empty way of life.

The externality of many Friends' lives, worsened by widespread ignorance of the elements of Christian faith and by the emphasis on outward practice as the measure of "soundness," created a crying need for renewal among Friends. In response to this need, two opposite tendencies in faith and thought began to emerge.

The doctrines of individualism, independent thought, and religious freedom, popularized in the late eighteenth century, strongly influenced some Friends. This was particularly true in America, where the popularity of the American and French revolutions and the influence of tracts such as Thomas Paine's *The Age of Reason* made freedom of religious belief an article of faith for many. Two expressions of these trends, one in Ireland

and one in America, gave evidence of the new thought and its influence on Friends.

In the final years of the eighteenth century, a number of Irish Friends, most notably Abraham Shackleton, began openly to deny the divinity of Jesus Christ and the veracity and authority of the Holy Scriptures. In their efforts to weed out heresy, Irish Friends disowned Shackleton and several ministers. Mass disownments and departures of Friends caused whole meetings to be laid down. The Irish schism was the largest separation that Friends had known.

Beginning around 1817, a group of New England Friends who styled themselves the "New Lights" denied the divinity of Jesus Christ and used claims of immediate inspiration to justify a variety of flamboyant and provocative behaviors (such as wearing swords to meeting). The New Lights rapidly disintegrated after most of their number were disowned for misconduct, but the outbreak of heterodoxy in the midst of the Society left many American Friends shaken.

These upheavals aroused some Friends, particularly in England, to a sense that Friends' doctrines must be upheld if the substance of Friends faith was to be preserved. These Friends, who eventually became known as the Orthodox party, were from the beginning a diverse group. Some were traditional Friends, concerned to uphold the "ancient testimonies" of the Society, with a renewed emphasis on a living faith founded on the indivisibilty of the inward and outward Christ. With Friends of earlier times, they sought to found their lives on obedience to the immediate guidance of the indwelling Christ. Others, particularly among wealthier and more educated Friends, were influenced by the Evangelical revival in the Protestant world. In addition to the atoning work of Jesus (important to all Orthodox), they emphasized the doctrine of justification by faith alone and the primary authority of the

Holy Scriptures. In time, the tensions between these groups would lead to the separations that produced a distinct body of Conservative Friends. For the time being, though, all were united in their concern to defend the Society's witness to Jesus Christ, which they saw to be at the heart of Friends' faith, against the inroads of infidelity. Allen and Richard Thomas summarize the beliefs that united Orthodox Friends:

> With some slight differences of opinion they held to the simple statements of the Gospels concerning the miraculous birth of Jesus Christ and to his essential oneness with the Father and with the Holy Spirit, though they preferred not to use the word Trinity as being non-scriptural. While not calling the Bible the "Word of God," which they reserved for Christ, they firmly believed in its inspiration. While the Spirit was primary, they maintained that the Scriptures bore testimony to the Spirit and the Spirit to the Scriptures, so that to be completely furnished both are needed. They held that the sacrifice of Jesus Christ on the cross was necessary for the sins of the whole world, and that through this sacrifice the gift of the Spirit is given to every man that cometh into the world. They believed that the light of Christ shone in the hearts of all and that every one would be judged according to the light given to him.[2]

An early evidence of Orthodox concern and influence was Philadelphia Yearly Meeting's adoption of a new Discipline in 1806, in which denial of the divinity of Jesus, the immediacy of divine revelation, or the authority of Scripture were made disownable offenses.

In America, Orthodox ministers' warnings soon focused on Elias Hicks, a popular minister of New York Yearly Meeting. Though he couched his sermons in Friends' traditional language, he at various times denied the divinity of Jesus Christ, the value of the atonement, and the inspiration of Scripture. Beginning with Stephen Grellet in 1808, a series of Orthodox ministers labored with Hicks or denounced his doctrine. The campaign against Hicks polarized American Friends into Orthodox and "Hicksite" parties. The Hicksites as a group were not so much believers in Hicks' doctrines as in individual freedom of religion. Many were orthodox Christians, but opposed the imposition of doctrine by religious authorities. Samuel Janney, who later became a prominent Hicksite minister and historian, wrote of the Orthodox:

> My doctrinal views at that time were similar to theirs; but I was so well assured that... other ministers, whose sentiments on some points differed from theirs, were good Christians, that I did not suffer myself to fall under the dominion of that censorious, uncharitable spirit which was laying waste our religious Society. The doctrines that I then held were those called Orthodox, but I could not endure the spirit of bitterness and party zeal by which those doctrines were too often accompanied.[3]

The Hicksites found support for their position in Friends' traditional opposition to religious creeds. Both Orthodox and Hicksite Friends opposed creeds, but for increasingly different reasons: Orthodox Friends felt that right doctrine was insufficient for a living faith, Hicksites that it was unnecessary.

The growing conflicts between the Hicksite and Orthodox parties finally led, in 1827 and 1828, to a convulsive schism that split five American Yearly Meetings (Philadelphia, New York, Baltimore, Indiana and Ohio), and permanently divided the Society into two groups, each claiming to be the true Religious Society of Friends. Since this history is concerned with the Orthodox branch, we will pass by the complex and unhappy story of this separation, and move on to developments among Orthodox Friends.

Histories of Friends during this period commonly attribute the rise of the Orthodox party almost exclusively to the influence of Evangelicalism on Friends. This view ignores the alarming effect that the New Lights controversy and the Irish separation had on traditional Friends, and discounts the great diversity of belief within the Orthodox camp. As a result, it gives little basis for understanding the separations that afflicted Orthodox Friends in following years, and that play such a large part in the history that follow[ed].

The Wilburite-Gurneyite Separation

The Hicksite separation did not restore peace among Orthodox Friends. Soon after the separation, a conference of delegates from all the American Orthodox Yearly Meetings was able to produce a common Declaration of Faith *(The Testimony of the Society of Friends on the Continent of America, 1830)*, but tensions within the Orthodox party soon became obvious.

As we have seen, the Orthodox included both traditional Friends, concerned to follow the promptings of the inward Christ in all things, and Evangelicals, who increasingly emphasized the importance of the outward work of Christ and the authority of the Holy Scriptures. Though these groups were united in their commitment to basic Christian doctrine, Conservative Friends suspected that the Evangelical doctrine of justification through faith alone was weakening Friends' understanding of the importance of a life sanctified in "bearing the cross." They saw a tendency among the Evangelicals to elevate the Holy Scriptures above the guidance of the Holy Spirit as a religious authority. They feared that these trends, if they became dominant, could undermine the foundations of Friends' belief. Ann Jones, a conservative minister, expressed these concerns at London Yearly Meeting in 1836:

> There are some among you who are encouraging a carnal wisdom, a head knowledge, an outward learning, which exalteth itself and is ever endeavouring, in its own strength, to find out the way of salvation by the study of Scripture. This spirit has spread even among those who are making a very high profession—men who are robbing Christ. They talk much of a belief in the atoning sacrifice but are at nought and despising Christ in his inward and spiritual appearance....The Lord hath a controversy with the spirit which hath crept into this Society, and which is sitting in the judgment-seat.[4]

Ann Jones was one of several ministers who had opposed the Hicksites, but now felt that Evangelical developments posed an equal and opposite threat to the Society. By this time, the Evangelical element had achieved such influence in London Yearly Meeting that her warnings, and those of other conservative ministers, had little effect.

Friends who sought to maintain the traditional doctrines of Friends were alarmed at London Yearly Meeting's general epistle for 1836, which for the first time presented the Evangelical views as the official position of Friends. A paragraph on the Holy Scriptures stated that they were "the only divinely authorized record of the doctrines of true religion" and "the appointed means of making known to us the blessed truths of Christianity." William Hodgson captures the Conservatives' objections to these statements:

> [They are] a direct abandonment of the principle always promulgated in [early Friends') writings, that "the appointed means" for the soul of man to obtain a saving knowledge of

God is a being taught in the school of Christ through obedience to the "Inspeaking Word," and faith in the revelations of
His Holy Spirit immediately in the heart; which will always
be *consistent with* Scripture.[5]

One of the first Americans to become concerned about
these trends was John Wilbur, a minister from South Kingston
Monthly Meeting in New England Yearly Meeting. A visit to
England in 1831-1833 exposed him to some of the most Evangelical ministers in London Yearly Meeting, and convinced him
that these ministers were beginning to rely less on the immediate guidance of the Holy Spirit in their ministry and everyday life than on their own strength and reason. He publicly
laid out his concerns in a series of letters to his friend George
Crosfield, published in England in 1832.

Wilbur blamed the new trends on the Hicksite separation. Some Friends, he said, had been so distressed by Hicksites'
elevation of "the Light," unchecked by Scripture or sound doctrine, that they had fallen into the opposite error of rejecting
the ultimate authority of the indwelling Spirit of Christ. They
had reacted to the Hicksites' slighting of Jesus Christ in the
flesh by focusing almost exclusively on Jesus' outward work.
They had reacted to the Hicksites' denigration of the authority of the Holy Scriptures by elevating the Scriptures above
Christ himself in authority. This swing toward the outward
aspects of Christianity had led them to rely on their own reason in the conduct of everyday life (for which the Holy Scriptures cannot give moment-by-moment guidance), with the
inevitable result that they were being led out into pride and
seduction by the world.

Wilbur was disturbed by the Evangelicals' campaigns for
religious education among Friends, such as the establishment
of First Day Schools, and by their willingness to cooperate

with non-Friends in Bible societies and reform projects. The first, he believed, would put Friends in the position of reaching religion according to a program, rather than according to the promptings of the Holy Spirit. The second would break down the hedge that protected Friends, particularly young Friends, from the seductions of the surrounding world.

Wilbur was prophetic in stating that this rejection of the primary authority of the Spirit of Christ would eventually undermine one of Friends' most basic testimonies, the immediate reliance on Christ's guidance in worship and ministry. In 1832, about forty years before the emergence of the pastoral system among some Friends, he wrote:

> ... if we as a people, were to change the place of the Scriptures, and exalt them above, and put them in the place of the teaching of the spirit of Christ, ... it must inevitably, and that before long, completely overturn and change our ancient faith and practice, concerning both silent worship, and the need there is of a continually renewed qualification in a gospel minister.[6]

Behind Wilbur's and the Conservatives' many particular concerns lay a fundamental one: that Evangelical Friends were acting in their own strength, rather than seeking a radical dependence on the immediate guidance of the living Christ.

All of Wilbur's concerns found a focus in the person of Joseph John Gurney, a wealthy and scholarly minister of London Yearly Meeting. In his many published writings, Gurney stressed the primacy of Scripture as a religious authority and the sufficiency of faith in Christ's atoning sacrifice for salvation; in public life, he encouraged cooperation between Friends and other Christians in Bible Societies and philanthropic work. Gurney had been instrumental in producing London Yearly

Meeting's 1836 statement on Scripture. To Wilbur, he seemed to personify everything dangerous in the Evangelical program. When Gurney visited the United States from 1837 to 1840, Wilbur privately communicated his concerns about Gurney's teaching to sympathetic Friends in New England and Philadelphia Yearly Meetings. Gurney, a polished speaker and an attractive personality, was greeted with great enthusiasm, and his tour of the American Orthodox Quaker world solidified the Evangelical tendency in most Orthodox Yearly Meetings.

In 1842, the leadership of Wilbur's own New England Yearly Meeting, solidly in sympathy with Gurney, ordered South Kingston Monthly Meeting to discipline Wilbur. Their claim was that an individual Friend (Wilbur) had no right to attack a minister in good standing (Gurney) except through Friends' disciplinary channels. When Wilbur's Monthly Meeting refused to comply, the Meeting was laid down by Rhode Island Quarterly Meeting and its members attached to another monthly meeting, which quickly disowned Wilbur. When Wilbur's appeal of this underhanded procedure to the Yearly Meeting was unsuccessful, he and about 500 supporters (less than ten percent of the total Yearly Meeting membership) withdrew to form a separate New England Yearly Meeting in 1845.

This separation imposed a crisis on all other Orthodox Yearly Meetings, which felt the need to decide with which New England Yearly Meeting they would remain in correspondence, and thus to declare themselves as "Wilburite" or "Gurneyite" in their allegiance. In the minds of Friends of the time, there could be only one undivided [Religious] Society of Friends. The acknowledgment of epistles from two New England Yearly Meetings was unthinkable; it was necessary to decide which was the real Yearly Meeting and correspond with it only. Being in correspondence with another Yearly Meeting was not simply a matter of exchanging epistles; it also determined whether membership could be transferred between Yearly Meetings, and whether traveling ministers would be received.

As in New England, New York Yearly Meeting's leadership and the majority of its members were Gurneyite in sentiment, and the Yearly Meeting quicky acknowledged the "Larger Body" in New England as the true New England Yearly Meeting. In response, separations occurred in several quarterly meetings beginning in 1847, and a separate, Wilburite, New York Yearly Meeting was first held in 1853. As in New England, it was much smaller than the Gurneyite body.

A pattern repeats itself in the polemical literature surrounding these separations: the Wilburites claimed that the defense of right doctrine was the fundamental issue while the Gurneyites claimed to be defending good order, and denied that doctrinal issues were central.

While Wilburites formed a small minority in New England and New York, the conservative element in Ohio Yearly Meeting outnumbered the Gurneyite group by about two to one. Thrown into crisis by the appearance of two New England epistles in 1845, the [Ohio] Yearly Meeting, clerked by the Wilburite Benjamin Hoyle, endured nine years of painful sessions in a struggle to maintain unity. The Gurneyite minority felt that Hoyle ignored their dissent and pushed through minutes of a Wilburite character over their protests. Nonetheless, Hoyle was repeatedly continued as clerk because the Yearly Meeting was unable to unite on a replacement. By 1853, things had come to such an impasse that virtually no business was transacted at Yearly Meeting sessions. The 1854 sessions were more heated than ever—literally, due to one of the hottest summers on record, and figuratively, due to the presence of both Thomas Gould, clerk of the Wilburite New England Yearly Meeting, and Eliza Gurney, widow of Joseph John. In this strained atmosphere, the Gurneyite group finally broke ranks and appointed its own clerk, Jonathan Binns. This act marked the separation of Ohio Yearly Meeting into two Yearly Meetings, which for years afterward were referred to as the "Hoyle" and "Binns" Yearly Meetings.

When London Yearly Meeting received epistles from two Ohio Yearly Meetings in 1855, it spent nearly three days deciding which Yearly Meeting to acknowledge. Though the Yearly Meeting was strongly Gurneyite, it recognized that the Gurneyite party had been out of order in appointing a new clerk. Allegiance finally won out over procedure, and the Binns Yearly Meeting was recognized. London Yearly Meeting's authority among Orthodox Friends guaranteed that most other Orthodox Yearly Meetings would follow suit.

At Baltimore Yearly Meeting's 1854 sessions a tiny separation occurred when the predominantly Gurneyite Yearly Meeting accepted the Binns party as the authentic Ohio Yearly Meeting. Six men and six women remained behind after the adjournment of the day's sessions and formed a Yearly Meeting in support of the Hoyle Ohio Yearly Meeting. This body, always very small, last met in 1868.

Philadelphia Yearly Meeting, like Ohio, had a substantial Wilburite majority. In 1847 the Yearly Meeting, over some opposition, distributed a 68-page *Appeal for the Ancient Doctrines*, a strong statement of what was coming to be called the the Wilburite viewpoint. When the separation occurred in Ohio, Philadelphia recognized the Wilburite group as the legitimate Ohio Yearly Meeting. This so dissatisfied the Gurneyite element in the Yearly Meeting that division seemed imminent. In 1857, the Yearly Meeting arrived at a drastic means of maintaining unity: it cut off formal correspondence with all other Friends bodies, neither sending nor receiving epistles. By this expedient the question of which other Yearly Meetings were to be recognized was avoided, and a separation was averted. Though it avoided taking sides organizationally, Philadelphia continued to be, in practice, a Wilburite Yearly Meeting containing a Gurneyite faction. The Wilburite and Gurneyite groups functioned almost as separate bodies, meeting in different meetinghouses and staying out of one another's way while retaining the fiction of a united Yearly Meeting. Frequent intervisitation between Philadelphia and the officially Wilburite bodies kept Philadelphia Yearly Meeting part of the Wilburite circle.

Concern for purity and unresolved questions over which Friends' bodies should be recognized continued to divide the Wilburite Yearly Meetings, all of which, except Baltimore, suffered further separations in the years following the Wilbur-Gurney schism. Two Wilburite groups quickly emerged. One, seeking to avoid division and to maintain unity with the larger [Religious] Society of Friends wherever possible, was hesitant to acknowledge other Wilburite groups established by schism. Ohio Yearly Meeting initially refused to acknowledge epistles or visiting ministers from any Yearly Meeting except Philadelphia (the only other Wilburite Yearly Meeting not established by separation). This put Ohio Yealy Meeting in the strange position of refusing to recognize the Wilburite New England Yearly Meeting, whose recognition had been the original issue leading to the Ohio separation. Philadelphia Yearly Meeting, along with Ohio, was guided by this outlook.

The other party, concerned with faithfulness at all costs to what they saw as the pure Friends tradition, were not averse to schism if it seemed necessary in order to preserve Friends' testimonies. They viewed the first group as compromisers, and derisively, labeled them "Middleites." Philadelphia Yearly Meeting came in for particular scorn for allowing a Gurneyite party to continue in its midst. The more purist party came to be called "Primitive" Friends for their unbending desire to preserve the "ancient testimonies" of Friends.

Fallsington General Meeting was first held in 1860, when about one hundred Wilburite Friends separated from Philadelphia Yearly Meeting and organized into two Monthly Meetings, Falls and Philadelphia. They condemned Philadelphia Yearly Meeting's refusal to acknowledge other Wilburite bodies, and believed that Philadelphia Yearly Meeting gave *de facto* approval to Gurneyite "Separatists" by routinely allowing transfers of membership between itself and Gurneyite Yearly Meetings. Fallsington General Meeting, though very small, served as something of a parent body to other Primitive groups, corresponding with them and accepting the members of meetings that died out. When the small Baltimore Yearly Meeting laid itself down in 1868, its one Monthly Meeting was attached to Fallsington General Meeting. At one time Fallsington had member meetings as far away as Iowa.

The small Wilburite New York Yearly Meeting suffered further separation in 1859, when some Friends broke away to form a very small Primitive body. The immediate cause of separation was a controversy over the publication of Joseph Hoag's *Journal*, from which the Primitive group wished to delete portions deemed critical of Job Otis, a zealous minister and not coincidentally a relative of several Primitive Friends. The deeper reasons for this separation are unclear, but in general the Primitive body ("The Yearly Meeting of New York," held at Poplar Ridge) wished to maintain unity with the "Smaller Bodies" such as Fallsington General Meeting, while the main body (which retained the "New York Yearly Meeting" title) was Middleite, seeking to achieve recognition by Ohio and Philadelphia Yearly Meetings.

The New York separation quickly spread to New England Yearly Meeting. In 1863, the Yearly Meeting declined to acknowledge epistles from Fallsington, Baltimore, or *either* New

York body on the grounds that these were schismatic meetings. The result was, of course, a division into two Yearly Meetings. The Primitive body, named the "Annual Meeting of Friends for New England," was concentrated in Nantucket, and Primitive Friends throughout New England joined Nantucket Meeting.

The Primitive New York and New England Yearly Meetings continued in correspondence with other Primitive bodies; the two Wilburite Yearly Meetings remained out of correspondence with every other Friends group including one another, rejecting the Primitive Yearly Meetings and rejected by the Middleite Yearly Meetings. The Wilburite New York Yearly Meeting died out around 1880. The fates of the other three will be told at a later point.

The Wilburites' belief that Yearly Meetings themselves established by schism should refuse to acknowledge "schismatic" groups seems comical at first sight, but did make some sense. Their position was that only doctrinal differences were a legitimate basis for separation. The separations that had produced the Wilburite Yearly Meetings involved (they said) questions of doctrine, while separations within Wilburite bodies were over points of order and should not be countenanced.

A notable virtue of the Primitive meetings was their refusal to enter into the bitter and degrading property disputes that typically marked divisions among Friends. These meetings were content to withdraw and attempt to start afresh, leaving behind without argument their former meetinghouses and even the names of their former Yearly Meetings.

Indiana Yearly Meeting was solidly Gurneyite, and did not undergo a separation at the Yearly Meeting level. A small separation did occur in several meetings in Iowa, then under the care of Indiana Yearly Meeting. The division began in 1854 at Lynn Preparative Meeting, which was made up largely of

Wilburite immigrants from Ohio Yearly Meeting.

Wilburite sympathizers in other meetings soon joined the separation leading to the formation of an independent Wilburite Salem Quarterly Meeting.

This group was severely weakened when Ohio Yearly Meeting established its own monthy meetings in Iowa, leading to the establishment of Hickory Grove Quarterly Meeting in 1867. Many in Salem Quarterly Meeting defected to meetings under Ohio's care, which seemed more legitimate because they were sanctioned by a yearly meeting. These departures led to the laying down in 1860 of one of the three monthly meetings in Salem Quarterly Meeting. The small remaining group underwent a Primitive separation in 1862. The Wilburite party apparently died out; the Primitive group joined Fallsington General Meeting in 1873.

In Ohio Yearly Meeting, a party of about fifty Friends, led by Joshua Maule, separated from the Yearly Meeting in 1863, again over the Yearly Meeting's refusal to recognize the other Wilburite Yearly Meetings. The "Maulite" group (officially Ohio General Meeting) itself divided in 1867, when the Maulite body failed to acknowledge an epistle from Fallsington General Meeting. The pro-Fallsington party withdrew, and most of its members joined Fallsington General Meeting. In 1870 Maule, his family, and a few others left the Maulite group, continuing to meet for worship in their own homes without any affiliation. Ohio General Meetiing disbanded in 1871, and most of its members returned to Ohio Yearly Meeting.

By about 1870, some stability had returned to the small world of Wilburite Friends. The two large Middleite Yearly Meetings, Ohio and Philadelphia, stayed close to one another through intervisitation, though official correspondence was ruled out by Philadelphia's policy. Three Primitive bodies (Fallsington General Meeting and the Primitive New England and New York meetings) kept fellowship with one another, while the two Wilburite Yearly Meetings in New England and New York continued in utter isolation. Except for Philadelphia Yearly Meeting, the Wilburites and Primitives were cut off from interaction with the larger [Religious] Society of Friends, though New England and Ohio Yearly Meetings, at least, had initially attempted to maintain correspondence and were rebuffed by most other Yearly Meetings, including London, whose rejection placed them officially outside the Orthodox Quaker pale. It is worth noting here that the Wilburite habit of isolation and withdrawal was originally imposed from without by other Yearly Meetings' rejection[s].

The Wilburites' genius for schism is sobering. Groups that were already small divided repeatedly for reasons that are difficult to understand today. Factions with only one Monthly Meeting styled themselves "Yearly Meetings" to lend authority to their position. The Wilburites' zeal for the preservation of fundamental Friends' testimonies seemed often to go along with a harsh and unbending spirit. The question of how a clear corporate witness can be fruitfully combined with a loving and reconciling spirit has never been resolved among Wilburite Friends.

Since Wilburite and Gurneyite Friends did not differ on most of the doctrines of the Christian faith, many have found their differences hard to understand. The Gurneyites themselves seem to have been perplexed at times: an Ohio Gurneyite said of the Wilburites in 1860, "No one can get any good reason for their bitterness out of them."[7] A modern Friend, even one with Conservative sympathies, might have difficulty distinguishing between the Wilburite and Gurneyite Friends of the 1840s and 1850s. All were orthodox Christians, all upheld the traditional Friends' ways of worship and ministry, all continued to live the plain life. Gurneyite Friends quickly moved to set up the First Day and Bible School classes so strongly opposed by Wilburites, but otherwise there was little outward difference between them. Ann Branson, a minister in Ohio Yearly Meeting at the time of the separation, recognized this similarity and viewed it as one of the dangers of Gurneyism for Friends:

> Gurneyism was a more specious snare to lay waste Quakerism, than ever Hicksism was. Hicksism is open infidelity, but Gurneyism is calculated to slide us off the foundation so imperceptibly that we shall not know it.[8]

Beginning in the 1860s, rapid changes in the Gurneyite world richly confirmed Wilburites' warnings of where Gurneyite doctrine would lead.

The 'Revival' Period

Three distinct groups emerged among Friends in the Gurneyite Yearly Meetings.[9] A small conservative group, committed to Friends' traditional testimonies on worship, ministry, and the plain life, would, for the most part, have been at home in the Wilburite Yearly Meetings.

A second group might be called "reform" Friends. These sought to encourage a more vital spiritual life among Friends by a cautious introduction of music, prayer meetings, and other innovative worship forms, and by a relaxation of the discipline (for example, eliminating disownment of Friends who married non-Friends). At the same time, they were committed to the waiting worship and inspired ministry that had always been central to Friends practice. The reform movement of the 1860s was successful in the sense that the decline in membership that all branches of Friends had experienced throughout the century was slowed and in some cases reversed.

In the 1870s, a third group of "revival" Friends, most of whose leaders had previously played no significant role in the Society, introduced methods, forms and doctrine taken from the Evangelical revival movement that was sweeping the Midwest at the time. Emotional testimonies, altar calls, and claims of instantaneous conversion and "holiness" experiences quickly came to characterize the meetings that they held among Friends and the general public. These revival meetings produced a large influx of new members and attendees into the midwestern Gurneyite meetings. Not surprisingly, these new members were confused by, and impatient with, the waiting worship of Friends meetings, so different from the revival meetings that had brought them to Friends. In an effort to manage the increase and hold on to the new members, Friends began to introduce formal pastoral leadership, arranged sermons, congregational singing, and other familiar features of Protestant services. In a short time, these innovations had rendered many Friends meetings outwardly indistinguishable from their Protestant neighbors.

At first, the Conservatives did not uniformly oppose the revivals. Several initially expressed cautious optimism at the new spiritual vigor that the revivals seemed to be introducing. When it became clear that the revival party was rapidly gaining control of the midwestern Gurneyite Yearly Meetings, and that the result would be the obliteration of Friends' former doctrines and practices, the conservatives vigorously opposed its innovations. By that point the revival movement had gained an unstoppable momentum, and the influence of Conservative Friends was swept aside along with that of the reform party.

Unlike the Wilburite separations of the previous generation, the Conservative separations that began in the 1870s were essentially reactions to the revival movement and the introduction of programmed, pastoral ministry that it brought with it. Except for North Carolina, all of the Yearly Meetings in which Conservative separations occurred had come into being after the separations of 1845-1854.

A revival meeting at Bear Creek Meeting (Iowa) in 1877 produced a separation that rapidly spread through Iowa Yearly Meeting. Thomas Hamm gives a vivid picture of this revival:

> Benjamin B. Hiatt… called on all who wished to lead a new life to come to the front seats. About twenty people scrambled forward, some climbing over the benches—Friends who remained at their seats were visited there by others and had prayer groups form around them. Some prayed aloud, some wept, some broke out in anguished testimonies, some sang snatches of hymns. Horrified, conservative Friends began to move toward the doors of the meeting house. As they did, one elderly woman climbed upon a bench and spoke in meeting for the first and only time in her life: "The Society of Friends is dead. This has killed it."[10]

Conservative Friends formed a separate Bear Creek Quarterly Meeting in Fifth Month 1877. Thus the Yearly Meeting, held later that year, received reports from two Bear Creek Quarterly Meetings. When the Yearly Meeting rejected the Conservative body's report, Conservative Friends withdrew and formed their own Yearly Meeting. Their opening minute summarizes the concerns of the Conservatives of this period:

> In consideration of many and various departures in Doctrine, Principle and Practice brought into our beloved Society of late years by modern innovators, who have so revolutionized

our ancient order in the Church as to run into views and practices out of which our early Friends were led, and into a broader, and more self-pleasing and cross-shunning way than that marked out by our Saviour, and held to by our ancient Friends... And who have so approximated to the unregenerate world that we feel it incumbent upon us to bear testimony against all such degenerate innovations in order to maintain our ancient Doctrines, Principles and Practices, and sustain the Church for the purpose for which it was so peculiarly raised up.[11]

In Western Yearly Meeting, revival meetings officially sanctioned by the Yearly Meeting began in 1871. In 1876, the Conservative leadership of Plainfield Quarterly Meeting closed down a revival held at Sugar Grove Meeting. When the resulting dispute was brought to the Yearly Meeting in 1877, the Yearly Meeting decided in favor of the revival party. Conservative members, seeing that their cause was lost, withdrew from the Yearly Meeting sessions. The first session of the Conservative Western Yearly Meeting was held in 1878, with some Friends from Indiana Yearly Meeting (which did not itself suffer an official separation) joining. The Yearly Meeting began with a First Day School Committee, a sign of how the new Conservatives differed from strict Wilburite thinking.

A separation in Kansas Yearly Meeting was again a response to revival meetings. The first Conservative Kansas Yearly Meeting sessions were held in 1879.

The separation in Canada Yearly Meeting was triggered by the proposed adoption of a revised Discipline, based on one adopted in 1877 by the Gurneyite New York Yearly Meeting, Canada Yearly Meeting's parent body. The revisions, which eliminated advocacy of plain dress and criticism of the "hireling ministry", came to Canada Yearly Meeting sessions for adoption in 1878. At the opening session, Adam Spencer, the conservative clerk of the Yearly Meeting, stepped down as clerk and withdrew from the Yearly Meeting. Other Conservatives followed his example over the next two years, and the first session of the Conservative Canada Yearly Meeting was held in 1881, in Norwich, Ontario.

Ohio Yearly Meeting, which had not recognized any of the earlier Wilburite separations, was more welcoming in its attitude toward the new Conservative Yearly Meetings. In 1881, the Yearly Meeting appointed a committee to consider "the situation of the remnants of Friends in various parts of the land." Members of the committee visited the new Yearly Meetings and in 1883 recommended that Iowa, Kansas and Western Yearly Meetings be acknowledged. The recommendation was "very fully united with" by the Yearly Meeting. In 1885, the Yearly Meeting united with the committee's recommendation that New England Yearly Meeting (the Wilburite branch) and Canada Yearly Meetings also be recognized.

The year after Iowa Yearly Meeting was recognized, Ohio Yearly Meeting began to consider transferring its Hickory Grove Quarterly Meeting, located in Iowa, to Iowa Yearly Meeting. This was finally accomplished in 1917, more than doubling the membership of Iowa Yearly Meeting. With the transfer, Scattergood School, established by Hickory Grove Quarterly Meeting, also came under the care of Iowa Yearly Meeting.

Another acquisition was Pasadena Monthly Meeting in California. A group of Conservative Friends had begun meeting for worship in Pasadena in 1886, and had been established as a Monthly Meeting by Hickory Grove Quarterly Meeting in 1894.

It is tempting to wonder whether early recognition of the

smaller bodies of Wilburite Friends by Ohio and Philadelphia Yearly Meetings might have helped to bring about a stronger, more united, and more influential Wilburite branch of the [Religious] Society of Friends. We might also wonder whether, if Orthodox Friends had not separated at all during this period, a Conservative presence could have prevented the wholesale departures from Friends' practice and belief that emerged in the Revival period. These questions are intriguing but unanswerable.

The North Carolina separation did not come until 1904, much later than the others. (By 1900, North Carolina was the only historic Yearly Meeting that had never suffered a separation, although Wilmington Yearly Meeting which was set off by Indiana Yearly Meeting in 1892 did not experience any separation.) The revival spirit and the pastoral system came into North Carolina later and more gradually than in the midwestern meetings, and thus polarization was less severe. By 1882, some Friends were objecting to revival meetings and a drift toward pastoral ministry. Their protests to the Yearly Meeting continued for twenty years, but never went so far as a separation. In 1890, these Friends asked, for reasons of conscience, to be excused from paying the portion of the Yearly Meeting budget devoted to evangelistic projects; the request was granted.

The immediate cause of schism was the attempt to introduce a "Uniform Discipline" in North Carolina Yearly Meeting. In 1902, most of the Gurneyite Yearly Meetings organized themselves into an umbrella organization, Five Years Meeting. Part of this process was the adoption of a Uniform Discipline by the member Yearly Meetings. Conservative Friends in North Carolina felt that the new Discipline encouraged the move toward programmed, pastoral worship, particularly by taking the recording of ministers out of the hands of Monthly Meetings and moving it to the Yearly Meeting level. When the Yearly Meeting adopted the Uniform Discipline in 1902, a group of Friends from Eastern Quarterly Meeting withdrew. They first met as a separate Yearly Meeting in 1904 at Cedar Grove Meeting in Woodland, North Carolina. Their minutes stated that they

> felt that it was right for them to maintain the doctrines of the immediate and perceptible guidance of the Holy Spirit, and of the Headship of Christ over all things to His Church; also the waiting worship and inspirational ministry which are and must ever be the outgrowth of these doctrines.[12]

All of the Conservative Yearly Meetings but Ohio acknowledged the new North Carolina Yearly Meeting immediately. Ohio Yearly Meeting moved more cautiously, but acknowledged North Carolina in 1911.

The separation in North Carolina, though painful, was accomplished with much less bitterness and social division than accompanied the other Conservative separations. Members of the two Yearly Meetings generally remained on good terms with one another, and at one point two brothers, Algie and Mahlon Newlin, simultaneously served as clerks of the two Yearly Meetings.

Ohio's acceptance of the new Yearly Meetings signified a broadening in its view of what constituted a faithful Friends' witness. Many of the new members might have been denounced as Gurneyites a generation before. On some points, such as their acceptance of religious education, most of the newer Yearly Meetings differed from the traditional Wilburite position. The new circle of seven Yearly Meetings (with Philadelphia an unofficial eighth) could now better be described as "Conservative" than "Wilburite." Conservative Friends were distinguished from other Orthodox Friends by their commitment to waiting worship and inspirational ministry and their continued adherence to aspects of the plain life. The more subtle differences between the Wilburites and Gurneyites of the 1850s had faded in importance in the face of the radical change that caused the wave of Conservative separations. Even among Conservatives, the traditional plain dress and speech were dying out by the turn of the century, though they continued to be the mark of a Conservative minister or elder well into the twentieth century and have never entirely disappeared.

The revival movement and the pastoral system never took hold in London Yearly Meeting, though the Yearly Meeting had been overwhelmingly Evangelical in sentiment throughout the 1800s. During the 1850s, the Yearly Meeting Discipline was relaxed, leading to a complete revision of the Discipline in 1860, in which the prohibition against marrying non-Friends was dropped, and the importance of plain dress and speech were greatly downplayed. Beginning in 1862, English Conservative Friends, united in their discomfort with Evangelical theology and their adherence to the plain way of life, began to hold a series of conferences several times a year for worship and mutual support.

The movement for separation was led by John G. Sargeant, who in 1864 moved to the village of Fritchley in Derbyshire and established a meeting there without seeking recognition by London Yearly Meeting. In 1868 Sargeant visited Wilburite bodies in the United States, where some American Conservatives encouraged him to establish a larger separate body. Back in England, Sargeant promoted his vision of an alternative to London Yearly Meeting at Conservative conferences in 1868 and 1869. Though the majority of English Conservatives chose to remain with London Yearly Meeting, a small group separated, and the first session of Fritchley General Meeting met in 1870, adopting London's *Discipline* of 1802 as its own. The General Meeting was always small, but slowly grew in numbers until at least 1900. Almost all of its members lived in or near Fritchley, though a meeting existed in Bournbrook, a suburb of Birmingham. A number of Friends moved to Fritchley or surrounding towns in order to be part of the Meeting.

Fritchley was unusual among Conservative meetings in maintaining an active dialogue with London Yearly Meeting Friends. John Sargeant visited and corresponded with "Friends of like mind" throughout England and Scotland, and several times was released by his meeting to witness among meetings not in unity with Fritchley. This practice was continued well into the twentieth century by other Fritchley ministers.

The Twentieth Century

After the many upheavals of the nineteenth century, the twentieth century was one of relative outward peace for Conservative Friends. Change went on, however, with a steady decline in numbers, the death or assimilation of all but three Yearly Meetings, and new questions of identity and the meaning of the Conservative witness in a changed world.

Following Ohio Yearly Meeting's acknowledgment of North Carolina Yearly Meeting in 1911, the seven Conservative Yearly Meetings enjoyed a period of harmony, united in polity practice and belief. In 1911, representatives of these Yearly Meetings meeting in Barnesville, Ohio, produced a *Brief Synopsis of the Principles and Testimonies of the Religious Society of Friends*. A clear summary of Conservative Friends beliefs at that time, it was adopted by all seven of the Yearly Meetings.

Unlike the Gurneyite and Hicksite Yearly Meetings, Conservative Friends have never formed a common organization. (In 1900 the Hicksite Yearly Meetings formed Friends

General Conference; in 1902 the Gurneyites formed the Five Years Meeting, already mentioned in connection with the North Carolina separation.) The 1911 conference that produced the Synopsis was probably the closest that Conservative Friends have ever come to officially coordinated action.

The First World War was a turning point in Conservative Friends' relations with other Friends' bodies and with the larger world. Conservative Friends were more united in their refusal to participate in war than were either the Hicksite or Gurneyite branches, and large numbers of young men endured the sometimes brutal conditions of the non-combatant camps run by the United States Army. In the camps, they found their convictions and sufferings shared by non-Conservative Friends as well as Brethren, Mennonites, and others.

In 1917, representatives of the Orthodox Philadelphia Yearly Meeting, Friends General Conference, and the Five Years Meeting founded the American Friends Service Committee (AFSC) to support and advocate for conscientious objectors, and to organize relief work in Europe. Conservative Friends supported the AFSC from the first, and gave generously to its first fund drive. Conservative Friends worked in AFSC's post-war relief programs in Europe, and returned with wider view of the world and other Friends.

The Second World War further increased cooperation with other Friends. Religious objectors to war were now able to work in Civilian Public Service (CPS) camps run by the traditional Peace Churches rather than by the Army. The AFSC organized and ran CPS camps for Friends, and Conservatives served in the camps or actively supported them. When the AFSC developed "CPS Fund Bonds" and "Peace Stamps" as alternatives to the government's Defense Bonds and Defense Stamps, students at Ohio Yearly Meeting's Friends Boarding School organized a drive to sell Peace Stamps. The era of shunning non-Conservative Friends and their organizations was clearly over.

The twentieth century saw the disappearance, through attrition or re-absorption, of four of the seven Conservative Yearly Meetings that had approved the 1911 Synopsis, as well as the Orthodox Philadelphia Yearly Meeting. Increased communication with non-Conservative Yearly Meetings paved the way for the reunion of three of these Yearly Meetings with bodies from which they had been separated for more than one hundred years.

Kansas Yearly Meeting, always small, dwindled to one Monthly Meeting, Spring River. The Yearly Meeting laid itself down in 1929, and Spring River Monthly Meeting joined Iowa Yearly Meeting in 1930.

Western Yearly Meeting laid itself down in 1962. Its only surviving Monthly Meeting, Plainfield, continued for some years as an independent meeting with loose ties to Conservative Friends, but eventually died out.

In 1945, New England Yearly Meeting joined with the (Gurneyite) Yearly Meeting of Friends for New England and with a number of independent Monthly Meetings to form a united Yearly Meeting.

Beginning around the time of the First World War, barriers between the Orthodox and Hicksite Philadelphia Yearly Meetings began to soften, as evidenced, by the Yearly Meetings' cooperation in projects such as the AFSC. In 1941, the two Yearly Meetings began holding joint business sessions in addition to their separate sessions. By 1950, nearly half of the Monthly Meetings in the Orthodox Yearly Meeting were "united" bodies, sharing membership in both Philadelphia Yearly Meetings. In 1955, the two Yearly Meetings formally united into one body.

Beginning in 1944, Canada Yearly Meeting met in joint

sessions with the Gurneyite Canada Yearly Meeting and Genesee Yearly Meeting (Hicksite); the minutes of the three Yearly Meetings were printed together. In 1955 the Yearly Meetings officially united to form Canadian Yearly Meeting.

The disappearance of these Yearly Meetings as distinct Conservative bodies left three surviving Conservative Yearly Meetings: Ohio, Iowa, and North Carolina. Though Kansas and Western Yearly Meetings died out for lack of numbers, New England, Canada, and Philadelphia were viable Yearly Meetings when they reunited with other Friends bodies. In all three cases, the reunions had been preceded by a long period of increasing closeness and work toward reunification. The bodies involved had come to feel that the differences between them had narrowed or faded in importance since their original separation. The near-disappearance of the plain life among Conservative Friends undoubtedly played a role: Friends could no longer point to differences in their ways of life as justifications for continued separation.

In New England and Canadian Yearly Meetings, the effect of the reunions was straightforward: the rapid disappearance of the Conservative witness, as if the Conservative Yearly Meetings that entered into reunion had been swallowed without a trace. The Conservative Yearly Meetings were substantially smaller than those that they joined—in New England, Conservative members were outnumbered by about thirty to one. Conservative Friends, characteristically slow and deliberate in their approach to decision-making, tend to be overrun by the relatively "fast" methods of other Friends. We need also to acknowledge that the Conservative Yearly Meetings had undergone substantial assimilation before reunion—and that this assimilation in large measure made reunion possible.

In Philadelphia Yearly Meeting, some Monthly Meetings that had maintained a Conservative identity before the

1955 reunion were able to continue as relatively Conservative meetings. It is clear, though, that the Yearly Meeting as a whole lost its Conservative identity. In 1954, the last year that the Orthodox Yearly Meeting held full sessions as a distinct body, its Minute of Exercise read, in part:

> If we open our hearts, God will open our whole being to testify to the Gospel of His Son....It is the heart of Jesus Christ that raises up in us Him who is able to do what we cannot do in our own strength. His is the testimony against all war, not ours. His is the testimony that we shall love one another. Knowing Jesus, we experience a profound repentance.[13]

Such a corporate testimony to Jesus Christ as our present Teacher and source of our strength has not been heard since from Philadelphia Yearly Meeting.

The handful of Primitive meetings that survived into the twentieth century continued to decline in numbers. Though the Primitive New York Yearly Meeting was laid down in 1896, its one surviving Quarterly Meeting (Scipio) continued independently for twenty years until it united with Canada Yearly Meeting in 1916. The Primitive branch of New England Yearly Meeting reunited in 1911 with the Wilburite branch, which had been part of the Conservative circle of Yearly Meetings since 1885. Fallsington General Meeting dwindled to one Monthly Meeting (Falls), which in 1950 rejoined Philadelphia Yearly Meeting's Falls Monthly Meeting.

Fritchley General Meeting took up official correspondence with London Yearly Meeting in 1937, and united with London in 1967. With the passing of its founding members, Fritchley General Meeting had become less distinguishable from other rural English meetings. London Yearly Meeting had changed also; the revival movement in America had shocked British Friends and broken the hold of Gurneyism on the Yearly Meeting, leaving it more appreciative of the Conservative position.

One of the factors in Fritchley General Meeting's decline was the departure of a large proportion of its membership (mostly members of Bournbrook Meeting) to Borden, Saskatchewan, beginning in 1904. In 1909, this group constituted itself as both Halcyonia Monthly Meeting and Western Canada Yearly Meeting. In 1937, Halcyonia Monthly Meeting joined Canada Yearly Meeting, and Western Canada Yearly Meeting disappeared. In 1955, when Canada Yearly Meeting joined in creating Canadian Yearly Meeting, Halcyonia Monthly Meeting did not feel clear to join in the reunion and withdrew. This isolated group still meets for worship.[14]

In 1915, a group of Conservative Friends from Ohio and Iowa who had settled near Fairhope, Alabama asked Stillwater Monthly Meeting of Ohio Yearly Meeting for authorization to set up a meeting for worship. Authorization was given, and after a few years as a Preparative Meeting, Fairhope Monthly Meeting was established in 1919.

In 1950 about half of Fairhope's membership moved as a group to Costa Rica. Disturbed by the military draft and increasing militarism in the United States, they chose Costa Rica because it had abolished its army in 1948 and was welcoming foreign settlers. The group settled a 3,000-acre tract of forested land, which they named Monteverde, in the mountains. In 1952, Monteverde Friends were released from membership in Fairhope Monthly Meeting at their own request and established an independent Monteverde Monthly Meeting.

Fairhope Monthly Meeting was badly weakened by the departure of the Monteverde Friends. After further declines in membership and diminished contact with Ohio Yearly Meeting, the meeting was laid down at its own request in 1967. The remnants of Fairhope Friends formed an independent Fairhope Monthly Meeting, which continues with greatly reduced contact with Ohio Yearly Meeting.

Throughout the twentieth century, many of the "ancient landmarks" that had distinguished Conservative Friends vanished. Some changes (such as the elimination of Friends' elementary schools) were driven by economic necessity; others (such as the abandonment of separate men's and women's business meetings) resulted from a deliberate decision that a practice had outlived its usefulness. In some cases (such as the abandonment of plain dress), change simply crept in over time without conscious choice.

At the beginning of the twentieth century, plain dress was disappearing; by 1950, it was rare. In Ohio Yearly Meeting, which changed most slowly, the Query on "plainness of speech and apparel" was answered year after year with phrases such as "Plainness of speech and apparel, as recommended by the discipline, is much neglected."[15] The revised *Book of Discipline* approved in 1963 finally dropped all mention of plain dress and speech, substituting the Query "Do we observe simplicity in our manner of living, sincerity in speech, and modesty in apparel?"[16] The great majority of Conservative Friends today dress simply and modestly, but are otherwise outwardly indistinguishable from their non-Conservative neighbors. For all but a few Conservative Friends, the plain speech has become an insider's language, used in the family and with other Conservative Friends, but not in conversation with the outside world.

Regular mid-week meetings for worship, held during the day on the fourth or fifth day of the week, were a powerful unifying force among traditional Friends. The effects of commerce and wage labor, along with increasing assimilation to the world, led to the decline of mid-week meeting, as a general practice among Conservative Friends.

Steady decline in membership led to the gradual closing of the primary schools once run by each meeting. Children's attendance at public school compromised the "guarded education" that had been so important in maintaining the integrity of the Conservative culture. When Stillwater Meeting in Ohio closed its primary school in 1941, it left only two primary schools in operation among Conservative Friends. The last surviving primary school, at Somerset Meeting in Ohio, closed in 1971.

Well into the 1930s, strict Conservative Friends continued to ignore the conventional Christian holidays, but enough families were observing them that, in 1928, Ohio Yearly Meeting's Boarding School for the first time scheduled its winter break to include "the day which the world calls Christmas."

Beginning with New England Yearly Meeting in 1907, all of the Conservative Yearly Meetings eventually began to meet in joint session—that is, without separate men's and women's meetings for business. (Meetings for worship had always been held jointly, though generally with women and men sitting on opposite sides of the meetinghouse.) Ohio Yearly Meeting, the last to change, held its first joint Yearly Meeting sessions in 1950.

The complex politics of sending and receiving epistles at last came to an end. Philadelphia Yearly Meeting began the process in 1897 when it sent a general epistle "to all meetings bearing the name of Friends." In 1934 Ohio Yearly Meeting resumed regular correspondence with non-Conservative Friends bodies. The typical practice now among the Conservative Yearly Meetings is to send individual epistles to other Conservative bodies, and a general epistle to all Yearly Meetings of Friends. The history of Friends might have been very different if this practice had prevailed in the nineteenth century.

A phenomenon unique to the twentieth century has been the proliferation of independent "unprogrammed" meetings, most of them urban or associated with college campuses. These meetings were often founded by Friends living at a distance from an established meeting, but they typically attracted members who were new to Friends. The Civilian Public Service camps in World War II and the civil rights and peace movements of the 1960s brought in newly convinced Friends with a strong concern for social action. The theology and spirituality of these meetings were strongly influenced by writers such as Rufus Jones and Howard Brinton, who characterized Quakerism as a form of Christian mysticism. Most meetings were liberal in theology, politics, and ethics. In many, Christian profession was no longer seen as a condition of membership, and some began to assert, for the first time in the history of any Friends body, that Quakerism was not essentially a Christian faith. Some of these meetings remained independent and unaffiliated. Some joined existing Hicksite Yearly Meetings, while others formed entirely new Yearly Meetings.

In Iowa and North Carolina Yearly Meetings, this movement produced an influx of new meetings, bringing both new energy and a substantially more liberal orientation. Although some traditional Conservatives felt uncomfortable with this new influence, it would be an overstatement to view it as a liberal invasion: those who joined Conservative Yearly Meetings were attracted to what they found in Conservative Friends, and were influenced by them.

Some of the social forces that helped the new meetings hurt the old ones. Conservative meetings were mostly rural, and were weakened by the twentieth-century shift in population from the country to the cities.

Of the eight Monthly Meetings now in North Carolina Yearly Meeting (Conservative) only two existed in 1945, and three of the five Monthly Meetings active in 1945 no longer exist. North Carolina Yearly Meeting has, in recent years, become a mixed body, with great diversity of outlook both within and between Monthly Meetings. Some North Carolina Friends adhere to the traditional theology of Conservative Friends and uphold remnants of the plain way of life; others participate in the liberal Piedmont Friends Fellowship and in Friends General Conference, the national body of historically Hicksite Yearly Meetings.

The effects of the new meetings were more dramatic and divisive in Iowa Yearly Meeting. Between 1960 and 1978, Iowa Yearly Meeting added seven new Monthly Meetings to its existing seven, though two were later laid down due to small membership[s]. Several of these new Meetings had been meeting independently since the 1930s or 1940s. The contrast between old and new came to a crisis in 1984, when John Griffith, the nominee for Yearly Meeting clerk, informed Yearly Meeting representatives that he was not a member of Friends (though a regular, attender), did not completely abstain from alcohol, and did not accept the atoning value of Jesus' death; he asked if, knowing this, they still wished to nominate him. The Yearly Meeting representatives reaffirmed the nomination. The nomination, and its widespread support, led to the withdrawal of Pasadena Monthly Meeting and the resignation of some Conservative members in other meetings.

New and wrenching social trends also left their mark on Ohio Yearly Meeting, most visibly in its painful eight-year consideration of same-sex marriages. When Cleveland Monthly Meeting, which had joined Ohio Yearly Meeting in 1966, proceeded in 1994 to approve the union of two women, its membership in the Yearly Meeting was discontinued by way of Salem Quarterly Meeting.

Beginning in the 1970s, Ohio Yearly Meeting in particular was affected by new Conservative influences. An increasing number of Friends, many of them "refugees" from liberal meetings, began to look to Ohio Yearly Meeting as a haven of traditional Christian Quakerism. A number of these Friends adopted plain dress and speech and a more classically Wilburite viewpoint than that of many long-time members of the Yearly Meeting. William Taber has characterized these Friends as neo-Conservatives. Friends who have adopted neo-Conservative ways remain few, but continue to be active and influential in Ohio Yearly Meeting. Small, unaffiliated meetings arising from the neo-Conservative movement also exist in New Jersey, Pennsylvania and Virginia.

London (now Britain) Yearly Meeting's steady departure from a Christian testimony in the 1980s and 1990s led to the formation of the "Yearly Meeting of Friends in Christ (Plain Quakers)" in 1993. This very small group, in the spiritual lineage of Fritchley General Meeting, comprises Friends from throughout the British Isles, and in 1996 united with Halcyonia Meeting in western Canada. Several of these Friends have adopted the plain life and describe them selves as "Primitive."

The Charismatic movement that swept through the Christian church in the 1960s and 1970s had its impact in Ohio Yearly Meeting, with complex results. The spiritual vitality introduced by the movement contributed to an increase in the number of recorded ministers, and imparted a more Evangelical style and content to much of the vocal ministry. Though some Charismatics left Ohio Yearly Meeting, many remained, and the Charismatic influence was to a degree incorporated into the traditional Conservative forms.

An increasingly important force for the preservation and

spread of the Conservative witness has been the series of General Meetings of Conservative Friends. The first of these was held at Friendsville, North Carolina in 1931. Another General Meeting in 1965, held in Barnesville, Ohio, included representatives of all existing Conservative bodies including Monteverde Meeting and Fritchley General Meeting. Since that time, the General Meetings have continued to be held every two or three years under the care of Ohio Yearly Meeting's Wider Fellowship of Conservative Friends Committee. The General Meetings now draw mostly members of Ohio and North Carolina Yearly Meetings, along with many visitors. Many have found in the fellowship and worship a fresh affirmation of the unique Christian testimony that Conservative Friends have upheld through the years. The announcement of the 1991 meeting, addressed to "Conservative Friends and others of like mind," speaks to the life yet to be found in this testimony: Our expectation is to gather under one Spirit in Christ Jesus, waiting in His Holy Covering and giving ministry under His Holy Unction, having our hearts and minds tendered, renewed with His peace that surpasses understanding.

1. *The Discipline of the Religious Society of Friends of Ohio Yearly Meeting* (Barnesville, Ohio: Ohio Yearly Meeting, 1922, 1963), p. 79.

2. Allen C. and Richard H. Thomas, *A History of the Friends in America.* Fifth ed. by Allen C. Thomas (Philadelphia: John C. Winston Co., 1919), p. 128.

3. Samuel Janney, *Memoirs of Samuel Janney* (Philadelphia: Friends' Book Association, 1881), p. 21.

4. William Hodgson, *The Society of Friends in the Nineteenth Century: A Historical View of the Successive Convulsions and Schisms Therein*

during that Period. Vol. 1 (Philadelphia: (no publisher), 1875-76), pp. 298-99.

5.*Ibid.*, p. 307

6.John Wilbur, *Journal of the Life of John Wilbur, a Minister of the Gospel in the Society of Friends; with Selections from his Correspondence, etc.* (Providence, Rhode Island: (no publisher), 1859), p. 592.

7. William Tallack, *Friendly Sketches in America* (London: A. W. Bennett, 1861), p. 76.

8. Ann Branson, *Journal of Ann Branson, a Minister of the Gospel in the Society of Friends* (Philadelphia: (no publisher), 1892), p. 228.

9.See Thomas D. Hamm, *The Transformation of American Quakerism: Orthodox Friends, 1800-1907* (Bloomington, Indiana: Indiana University Press, 1988), pp. 99-120.

10.*Ibid.*, pp. 84-5.

11.Darius B. Cook, *Memoirs of Quaker Divide* (Dexter, Iowa: The Dexter *Sentinel,* 1914) pp. 85-6.

12.Kenneth S. P. Morse, *A History of Conservative Friends* (Barnesville, Ohio: by the author, 1962), p. 50.

13.Philadelphia Yearly Meeting, *Minutes* (Philadelphia: Philadelphia Yearly Meeting, 1954), p. 29.

14.Mary Hinde, personal communication.

15.Ohio Yearly Meeting, *Minutes* (n.l.: Ohio Yearly Meeting, 1935), p. 7.

16.*The Discipline of the Religious Society of Friends of Ohio Yearly Meeting,* p. 23.

Appendix D

Conservative Friends Yearly Meetings and Related Resources

Iowa Yearly Meeting (C)
Deborah Fisch
916 41st Street
Des Moines IA 50312

North Carolina Yearly Meeting (C)
Deborah Shaw
1009 W. McGee Street
Greensboro NC 27410

Ohio Yearly Meeting (C)
Correspondent: Dorothy Smith
61830 Sandy Ridge Road,
Barnesville OH 43713

Wider Fellowship of Conservative Friends
c/o Nancy Hawkins
409 S. Walnut Street
Ravenna OH 44266

Center for Plain Living
60805 Pigeon Point Road
Barnesville OH 43713

Index

TRuth XVI

The Coopers Today

Wil and Emily Cooper now live at Friends Fellowship Community in Richmond, Indiana, during warm months and winter in Palm Harbor, Florida on the Gulf Coast. There they live in Southwind Mobile Home Park near their son Scott and his family in the Tampa Bay area. He and Lori have two boys and a recently adopted Chinese daughter—Wilmer and Emily's first granddaughter! Scott is a telecommunication engineer and is president of Vela Research, which designs and markets high-tech television and computer equipment.

Their three daughters live in the general area of Boston, Massachusetts, where Wilmer and Emily visit at least once a year. One of the families has a cottage on Cape Cod where they usually go for a week or two in the fall. Suzanne Cooper lives in Boston and is a registered nurse and muscular therapist. Cathy is married to Richard Papazian, director of administrative computing at Tufts University in Boston. The Papazians have two sons and live in Lexington, Massachusetts, where Cathy is a social worker. Barbara is married to Roland Bartl, whom she met on Earlham foreign study in Heidelberg, Germany. The Bartls have two sons and live in Gardner, Massachusetts, west of Boston. Barbara is an occupational therapist in Leominster hospital, and Roland is town planner in nearby Acton.

In addition to Emily's work as a nutritionist for the WIC program, in recent years she has become an avid quilter in Richmond and in Palm Harbor. In Florida she joined a quilting guild and also teaches quilting in the community where they live. Her quilting will be remembered most for a large wall quilt named "The Lion and the Lamb Shall Dwell Together in Peace," commissioned by the Earlham School of Religion. It now hangs on the wall in the Gathering Room at the school.

Wilmer and Emily Cooper Family

Top row (from left): Cathy (Cooper) Papazian, Rich Papazian, Susanne Cooper, Roland Bartl, Barbara (Cooper) Bartl, Scott Cooper. Middle: Chris Papazian, Emily Cooper, Wilmer Cooper, Jonathan Cooper, Lori Cooper. Bottom: Nathan Papazian, Stefan Bartl, Daniel Bartl, Timmy Cooper, Elizabeth Xioming Cooper. (Photo 1994; Elizabeth, born in 1997, was added by photo magic for this publication.)

WILLIAM AND FRANCES TABER, members of Ohio Yearly Meeting (Conservative), are active members of the Religious Society of Friends. They have been intimately involved with Olney Friends Boarding School—first as students and later on the teaching and administrative staff. For thirteen years the Tabers lived and worked at Pendle Hill, a Quaker center for study and contemplation near Philadelphia. There Bill Taber taught courses in Quaker studies and prayer, and Fran developed a personal retreat program. The Tabers now live in their home in Barnesville, Ohio, where they are active in Stillwater Monthly Meeting, Ohio Yearly Meeting, and Olney Friends School. Fran is a teacher in the School of the Spirit. Together Bill and Fran have helped develop a new Friends Center at Olney Friends School.

JOHN BRADY was for many years an active member of the Religious Society of Friends, first in New England Yearly Meeting, then in Ohio Yearly Meeting. His pamphlet, *A Short History of Conservative Friends*, is condensed in Appendix C of this book. John and Marilyn Brady and their son Joel live in Barnesville, Ohio, where they are members of the Eastern Orthodox Church.

Also Available

Friends United Press

A Living Faith by Wilmer A. Cooper
Encounter with Silence by John Punshon
Inner Tenderings by Louise Wilson
John Woolman, 1720-1772 by David Sox
The Journal of George Fox, edited by Rufus M. Jones
The Journal and Major Essays of John Woolman,
    edited by Phillips P. Moulton

Pendle Hill Publications

A Certain Kind of Perfection by Margery Post Abbott
*A Description of the Qualifications Necessary to a
    Gospel Minister* by Samuel Bownas
*Hidden in Plain Sight: Quaker Women's Writings,
    1650-1700,* by Dortha Meredith, Mary Garman,
    Judith Applegate, and Margaret Benefiel
Love Is the Hardest Lesson by Margaret Hope Bacon
Love at the Heart of Things: A Biography of Douglas Steere
    by Glenn Hinson
The Quaker Reader by Jessamyn West